I0759558

The Home Bird

Creating Joyful Interiors Where Old Meets New

Elle Hervin

MITCHELL BEAZLEY

A LITTLE LIFE
HELLO BEAUTIFUL
SIX DAYS
TAPE
DEAD ENDS
HOW TO BE FAMOUS
LUCKY
BUTTER

CONTENTS

Introduction

A Love of Interiors: The Journey

Even as a little girl, I had a fascination for quirky and characterful homes; whether it was the idiosyncratic apartment of my mother's artist friend, a stately historic house we visited as children, or a tiny country cottage where we spent a rather rustic family holiday, these were spaces that fuelled a curiosity and piqued an interest from a young age. Somewhere along the way, this subconscious draw to distinctive spaces developed into a passion for interiors, which has followed me into adulthood. Growing up with a mother who was a painter and ceramicist and a father who had a penchant for Persian rugs and European pottery, I was exposed to all kinds of creative expression in my formative years, but really, I would say it was my grandparents' colourful and layered home that fuelled a lifelong love of vintage interiors and inspired my own home decor style.

Some of my happiest childhood memories are of time spent at my grandparents' characterful home; there were rooms filled with objets d'art, large oil paintings of some distant ancestor, vintage board games, dusty old books, and precious antiques. It was a place that felt simultaneously magical and comforting, with nostalgia at its core. My granny's keen eye for quality vintage style meant their home was a mixture of grandeur and understated elegance. It was an aesthetic that created an interesting juxtaposition with the 1980s property they lived in, a building lacking in any kind of period features or architectural merit, but somehow my grandmother managed to elicit a sense of old-world charm within a contemporary building. Old meets new is an approach to interior design that has been at the heart of my own decorating style and embodies the very essence of *The Home Bird: Creating Joyful Interiors Where Old Meets New.*

Creating a Healing Home

Stockpiling interiors magazines and pouring obsessively over paint colours has been an unabashed habit for most of my adult life, but little did I know that my love of interiors and vintage decor would go on to save me in many ways. During childbirth with my youngest son, now seven, I almost lost my life due to a very rare complication; a terrifying experience that left me with PTSD and led to a cycle of severe anxiety, insomnia and stress. Ironically, it would be the gargantuan stress of a large-scale renovation the following year that kickstarted my recovery from trauma. I developed an innate need to design spaces that not only felt safe and nurturing for myself and my family, but also to create a home that held a little joyful magic in every room.

Searching for secondhand and vintage homewares became a therapy of sorts and allowed me to see how curating an individual home could be both healing and hugely enjoyable; I discovered a cathartic kind of beauty in repurposing a neglected, unloved piece of furniture from a flea market or car boot sale (swap meet). Taking a more organic approach to sourcing furniture also felt intrinsically purposeful and, in many ways, more responsible; there is much

CLASSIC & CONTEMPORARY Vintage Thonet bar-stools sourced on eBay create a warm contrast against vibrant blue, Shaker-style kitchen cabinets and granite countertops in my kitchen, while egg-and-dart cornicing from Plaster Ceiling Roses adds traditional detail, as do Art Deco-style globe pendant lights. A collection of ceramics and old enamel storage bins adds interest to shelves and cupboards.

BREAD
ANISETTE

gratification to be gleaned from actively rejecting mass-produced furniture in favour of secondhand pieces and, in turn, embracing a more sustainable and eco-friendly way of furnishing your home. Uncovering the joy of curating more mindful spaces in my home has led to a passion for exploring how we can develop a greater emotional connection to the spaces we occupy. This can be achieved through authenticity-driven interior design and the inclusion of nostalgic decor, and by creating characterful, nurturing spaces that better reflect who we are.

Me, My Home and Social Media

You could say that it was a natural progression; my accidental journey into online content creation was maybe less of an accident and more of a foregone conclusion, having worked in journalism and other creative niches for over a decade. An unshakeable need to be artistic has always been the driving force behind whatever I do, whether it be writing, photography or, in more recent years, producing content for interior and lifestyle brands. Something I did not predict, however, was the success of my social media journey, namely my Instagram account @elle_the_home_bird; now with one million followers, my page has become a source of interior inspiration to hundreds of thousands of people around the world.

I often wonder why this is. I'm not a trained interior designer, nor do I profess to be the world's greatest at DIY, but therein lies the attraction, I suppose; an ordinary mum-of-three who turned an average semi-detached house (duplex) into something a little less average by creating corners that have captured the imaginations of like-minded souls. On my social channels, I am asked daily for advice, tutorials and how I created my decor schemes, and so, after many years, I'm finally sharing my top tips, sources of inspiration and the formula behind my modern vintage aesthetic – all within *The Home Bird*.

A Book for Interiors Lovers, Homebodies and Everyone In Between

This is a book for those wanting to create a little magic in their home interiors, who dream of charming, characterful spaces unique to them and whose love of decor transcends mere aesthetics to encompass how spaces *feel*. It is an indispensable compendium for lovers of vintage, for those wanting tips on blending contemporary with classic decor, and also interiors enthusiasts who are simply passionate about beautiful design, all while offering inspiration through the most remarkable of homes showcased within these pages.

In *Part One – Curating Joyful Interiors*, I share my 7-step formula for creating a modern vintage aesthetic, along with advice on how to inject your home with joyful decor and turn ordinary areas into extraordinary spaces. *Part Two – Rooms to Inspire* takes a room-by-room look at how to design beautiful, yet practical interiors, while in *Part Three – Homes to Inspire*, I take you on a tour of nine beautiful, individual and inspiring homes, including a rustic Australian cottage where time has stood still, a mid-century apartment within a fairytale tower, and an eclectic, bohemia-inspired artist's residence, and many more joyful homes in between.

INTERIOR INSPIRATION The muted pink walls of my bedroom, painted in Farrow & Ball's 'Setting Plaster', are complemented by a striking vintage suzani sourced on Etsy and a traditional brass bed from the Cornish Bed Co. It is one of many spaces that I share with my followers on my social media channels, which have attracted interiors enthusiasts from across the world.

COOKERY
HOUSEHOLD MANAGEMENT
LITTLE WOMEN

PART ONE
Curating Joyful Interiors

Curating an Authentic Aesthetic

There is untold charm to be found within a home where personality percolates through joyfully curated decor, where spaces are filled with idiosyncrasy, and curiosity is awakened at every turn. This is the epitome of an authentic aesthetic – favoured design styles peppered with one's own personal preferences, offering a glimpse into the inhabitants' inner world and enshrouding spaces with warmth and comfort. Good 'bones' come from architectural features, but real character comes from deeper within: the manifestation of one's passions, dreams and unfiltered eccentricities.

A line of old hardback books sits atop an elegant 1800s desk once belonging to my grandmother; their faded, yet colourful spines create a muted rainbow of blues, reds and greens. What they lack in lustre, they more than make up for in charm and character. A vibrant blue lamp and contemporary brass candlesticks complete the vignette, the juxtaposition between old and new creating contrast and intrigue in an otherwise ordinary corner of the living room.

I am often asked how to put together a modern vintage 'look' similar to this one and how to create an aesthetic that feels lived in, yet refined. For me, the answer lies in the peaceful elegance that older pieces bring to a space combined with the youthful energy of more contemporary accessories; even though they are seemingly at odds with one another, when successfully blended they create serendipitous harmony. By dovetailing flea market finds and vintage treasures with one or two newer pieces, it has given me the freedom to be playful with my interiors and embrace the versatility of this rather nonchalant style of decor.

Nonetheless, achieving a natural and authentic aesthetic requires a little more consideration than merely collecting items with unmitigated abandon, which can be tempting, I know. Creating a home that tells the story of who you really are – your passions, aspirations, travels and experiences – lies in curating meaningful items that hold emotional and sentimental value for you, along with those pieces you pick up simply because they are too joyful to resist. Your home should be a living, breathing memory book of sorts.

The most gratifying part of creating a modern vintage aesthetic that is truly organic lies in the very process of collecting and curating, often over many years. Think of it as an ever-evolving journey rather than a destination to be reached as quickly as possible; a slow-moving but still thrilling merry-go-round of sourcing, accumulating and experimentation.

AT HOME WITH CHARACTER An original mid-century painting creates a focal point in my modern vintage living room, while contemporary accessories, including a vibrant blue lamp base from Pooky Lighting and linen lampshade from Alice Palmer & Co, add a playful element to the aesthetic. Walls painted in Benjamin Moore's 'Hamilton Blue' are complemented by brass and red accents.

My 7-Step Formula for Creating a Modern Vintage Home

There is a danger that a collected interior, if left unchecked, can become more of a chaotic jumble of 'junk' than a meaningful collection of objets d'art. Curating character that's cohesive involves having a common thread running throughout your home tying everything together, with **recurring themes** and a **controlled colour palette**. This ensures intentional spaces exude personality but avoid resembling a car boot sale (swap meet).

The more interior schemes I create and implement, the more I've come to realize that spontaneity in design can be a frustrating time- and money-waster. It pays to pause for a moment, jot down some ideas, experiment with mood boards and take a measured approach to the space as a whole. I often start with my inspiration for a room before slowly working my way up to a design scheme that includes furniture, accessories, artwork and lighting.

Creating a beautiful home does not require a degree in interior design, but having a simple toolkit can help you filter through the often overwhelming plethora of design advice, inspiration and fleeting trends we all find ourselves bombarded with on a daily basis. To simplify the process, I have created a 7-step guide to curating a cohesive and authentic home interior and have included a few top tips along the way.

Step

1

Inspiration

Identify your favourite design styles

- Take inspiration from places you've visited, maybe a restaurant or shop interior that has stuck in your mind, along with images from Instagram, Pinterest and interiors magazines.
- Organize your inspirational ideas into 'collections' for each room and mood board ideas. (Top tip: I love Canva for its simple mood board templates.)
- Identify what you love about those things that inspire you – the colours, style period, furnishings, accessories and lighting.

Step

2

Colour

Create a unifying colour palette

- Identify colours you're drawn to, or take inspiration from a favourite item of decor such as a sofa, rug or piece of artwork.
- Restrict your palette to three to five colours and then use variations of these in similar tones around your home.
- Add a complementary accent colour and carry this into your space through accessories such as cushions, throws and artwork.

For more on how to use colour in your home, see pages 24–29.

Step

3

'Red Thread' Theory

Introduce a common design thread throughout your home

- Considered the holy grail of successful interior design, introducing a common design element throughout your home can help tie together all the spaces.
- You can achieve this through colour (it doesn't have to be red!), shape and texture, along with accessories and furniture.
- You can have more than one 'red thread'. (Top tip: I use brass elements in almost all my rooms, plus a consistent use of the same accent colour.)

Step

4

Pattern and Texture

Create layers of interest with whimsical fabrics and wallpaper

- Add layers of interest in your home through textured elements, fabrics and pattern.
- Use patterned wallpaper in a floral or whimsical design. (Top tip: small-scale prints tend to look more 'vintage', while larger-scale prints feel more contemporary.)
- Add cushions and bedspreads with heritage, traditional or nostalgic fabrics. (Top tip: use more than one pattern but pick a 'hero' or showstopper print as the dominant pattern.)

Step

5

Furniture

Layer antique or secondhand furniture

- Include antique and vintage wooden furniture to add warmth, authenticity and character.
- Don't be afraid to mix pieces from different styles or periods of design – this can create a fresh and interesting juxtaposition.
- Do consider scale – balance heavier pieces with lighter, leggier items and give items room to breathe, so the space doesn't look too chaotic.

For more on buying vintage furniture, see pages 30–39.

Step

6

Artwork

Choose a varied selection of artwork you're drawn to

- An essential finishing touch, art is instrumental in elevating your interior and adding interest and individuality to your home.
- Choose from vintage poster prints, oil paintings, botanical sketches, black-and-white photographs, antique maps and illustrations from vintage books. (Top tip: Etsy has lots of affordable prints and also check charity shops for old paintings and frames.)
- Mix a few different styles to create a dynamic, eclectic collection. (Top tip: including artwork with colours from your chosen colour palette helps create cohesion and consistency.)

Step

7

You

Make your home meaningful and reflective of who you are

- Take inspiration from but don't copy someone else's interiors piece for piece – it will hold little meaning for you and you will quickly fall out of love with it.
- Take time getting to know what you love and how your interior spaces make you feel – this will result in more meaningful choices when it comes to your home decor.
- Choose only things you really love, those that evoke happy memories or you've collected over time.

THE ST IVES ARTISTS
THE ST IVES ARTISTS
CHRISTOPHER WOOD
The Art of Bloomsbury
RICHARD SHONE

THE IMPRESSIONISTS
The Impressionists
WILLIAM MORRIS

The Dopamine Decor Effect

Mood-boosting decor that infuses spaces with an ebullient energy can be found in a concoction of colour, pattern and whimsical details that either define a design scheme or are sprinkled sparingly throughout the home.

Patterned wallpapers, bold paint colours, vintage fabrics and colourful accessories all fall under the concept of 'dopamine decor', a phrase used to describe a style of decoration that injects your home with character, while giving you that heady, feel-good factor. Like any approach to interior design, however, dopamine decor will look and feel different for each individual, and personal preference should reign when incorporating these elements into your own aesthetic. As a loyal and dedicated devotee of colour and pattern, I've tried to include both in most (if not all) the spaces in my home to varying degrees, but I try to exercise some restraint, so as not to overwhelm a scheme.

Dopamine decor in your own home could be as simple as including some patterned cushions on a plain sofa, or adding a vintage bedspread to the bedroom, or if you're feeling brave, adorning the walls with a bright paint colour. Rather than focusing on creating a specific style of decor, concentrate more on what brings you joy and makes you happy; look for meaningful pieces that either hold some emotional connection or simply spark that giddy feeling you get when you see something you love.

COLOUR CONCOCTION A bold wall colour such as Farrow & Ball's 'Fruit Fool' creates an uplifting and exuberant aesthetic, especially when paired with colourful fabrics and accessories (previous pages). Darker colours, such as a deep blue painted on the walls in 'Hamilton Blue' by Benjamin Moore, can feel both cosy and immersive (left).

MOOD BOOSTING Patterned cushions, decorative fabrics and wallpaper introduce colour and interest to a space, infusing it with a characterful, feel-good energy. A bold wallpaper defines a room, while a pile of patterned cushions can add a subtle sprinkling of colour to a more neutral aesthetic (opposite).

Making Ordinary Spaces Extraordinary

The secret to creating captivating interiors, layered with intrigue and originality, often lies in the quiet curation of those unassuming and seemingly unimportant corners of our homes; spaces where unexpected interest and personality can be forged.

Just like our day-to-day lives when small moments can feel inconsequential, we often overlook the minor details of our homes and focus on the bigger picture, but if you were to zoom in on your life, it would often be those ordinary events that held the most significance, and the same is true of our homes. As the old adage says, the devil is in the detail.

We often disregard many areas of our homes, such as the hallway table where we throw our keys or the mail, as insignificant, maybe because they operate merely as functional spaces. But these little corners can provide just as much opportunity as more obvious spaces for creating character. Here are some 'ordinary' spaces which you can easily make a little more extraordinary.

Kitchen shelves are one of my favourite places for creating unexpected visual interest. Cluster plates, pots and artwork of varying sizes and heights in threes, along with a vase filled with foliage, and you have instant colour and character. Top tip: Arrange items in ascending or descending height order to create a triangle shape; this is more aesthetically pleasing to the eye.

The **mantelpiece**, usually home to the odd family photo and maybe an ornament or two, is a central focal point that's often overlooked when styling the home. For elevated mantelpiece decor, add some candles (I have a thing for the twisted ones in pastel hues), a vase of flowers and a statement ornament such as a vintage model sailing boat for a subtle suggestion of whimsy and nostalgia.

An **alcove** can create an evocative scene reminiscent of a still-life painting in a corner of the living or dining room. Include items that hold meaning or bring you joy, but don't overload the space; give each item room to breathe. A vintage side table with a lamp, a few antique books and a vase with some greenery feels relaxed, yet curated. Top tip: Include items that pick out the main room colours to achieve a consistent colour palette.

The **bathroom cabinet** can add real character to what is another functional room. If space allows, include either a freestanding or wall-mounted cabinet with some simple styling, such as a few amber glass bottles filled with your favourite products alongside a vase of flowers, to instantly draw the eye and create a little moment of magic in a corner of this room.

The **hallway table** can be prone to gathering clutter, but if utilized well, this humble table can be home to essential, yet unaesthically pleasing, items as well as a little bit of dopamine decor. I love using a statement table lamp along with a big vase of flowers; it feels like a simple, yet welcoming, prelude to my home.

For more styling tips throughout the home, see Part Two – Rooms to Inspire, pages 40–83.

UNEXPECTED INTEREST Oversized hand-painted stripes create a striking backdrop to these alcove bookshelves, which have been painted in a harmonizing green. Stacked with a casual curation that allows both useful and decorative items to sit side by side, they invite the eye to roam over the various curios on display, while transforming the space from ordinary to interesting.

MASTERING ARTISAN CHEESEMAKING ● CALDWELL
THE SILVER SPOON
Perfect Houseplants
Willow Crossley
Flourish.
The Victory Garden Cookbook
Marian Morash
Olives
a platter of figs and other recipes
DAVID TANIS
the great vegetable plot sarah raven

Blending Classic & Contemporary

Influenced by art, travel and nature, interior designer **Lucy Cunningham** takes a colourful, layered approach to interior design schemes, where modern additions collide peacefully with historically inspired designs.

Signature style? A refined English aesthetic in which the contemporary and classic are blended seamlessly, with colour and pattern at the heart of design schemes.

What do you love about using colour and pattern in a design scheme? In all the projects I work on, I try to create a cosy and homely feeling, something warm and inviting that makes you want to stay in that room. I find colour and pattern to be so uplifting, warming and happiness-making; people just want to feel joyful in their homes.

How do you use colour to create a certain 'mood' in a space? I love using warmer colours such as ochres, burgundies and greens; they have a soothing effect on the atmosphere of a room.

What's your approach to mixing classic and contemporary styles? Interior design 'rules' are being left behind somewhat; nowadays people are excited to experiment and break the rules. Putting modern and vintage together is just one of the many things people are doing to explore and test the boundaries of design. Often, the braver I am, the better the result.

How important is authenticity in how we decorate our homes? Authenticity is important for me; I want a home to feel like a home, a lived-in space that can be enjoyed by everyone in it and not just a show home. People are thinking a lot more about how they live, what makes them happy in a home, and what works practically for them.

What does using older or vintage pieces in our home bring to a design scheme? People are starting to recognize the value and interest in older pieces, the period of time they come from, and what they represent. Older furniture helps to bring depth to a space and is wonderful in the layering of a room; I love putting a dark piece of furniture in a space to ground the scheme. It's also a lot of fun to inject some personality into a room by adding older pieces.

MIX IT UP Decorative plates, vintage ceramics and curios that catch the eye can be displayed on shelves and mantelpieces. Even a spare space on an empty wall can be used for an idiosyncratic blend of old and new. Small collections of meaningful trinkets add depth and interest to both colourful and more neutral backdrops, as seen in the examples opposite.

The Joy of Colour

Colour is at the very core of joyful decorating and its transformative power knows no bounds; rooms once cold and impersonal become spaces filled with an invisible energy, an effervescence of sorts, and gain a personality of their own.

Colour can evoke a profound emotional response, rouse memories and breathe new life into a space. The mood we want to create in a room can inform our colour choices, whether it be cosy and comforting using darker tones, or zestful and invigorating with brighter hues. Breaking away from the confines of conventional decorating, such as keeping the ceilings and woodwork white, can also afford us creative freedom with how we use paint colours; colour-drenched ceilings, bright woodwork and bold colour pairings create exciting spaces that feel multifaceted.

Colour-drenching the plaster-pink walls and ceiling of my bedroom has created a cocoon-like sensation in a space that was previously cold and lifeless. Painting this dark, shady room in Farrow & Ball's 'Setting Plaster', a soft, muted pink, was the catalysis for my now boundless enthusiasm for experimenting with paint colours. My bedroom was transformed by colour but it also made me *feel* a certain way: comforted, relaxed and peaceful. From that point onwards, I've been hooked on the emotional power of colour.

So, how can you incorporate more colour into your home? Colour can be injected into a space in a number of ways, from painting the walls a bold or bright colour to more subtle additions through the use of colourful accessories and artwork.

Five Ideas for Adding Colour to Your Home

1 *Patterned cushions* – floral, geometric, striped, kantha (cushions or quilts stitched using layers of traditional Indian garments) and suzani (traditional embroidered textiles).

2 *Painted chairs* – paint old wooden dining chairs in your accent colour for an instant injection of colour and personality.

3 *Artwork* – I love Swedish abstract expressionist art for its use of colour, but a vibrant vintage poster print works just as well.

4 *Rugs* – try a Persian kilim or Bijar rug, a traditional oriental rug, or a geometric design for added vibrancy, texture and colour.

5 *Ceramics and accessories* – vases, jugs (pitchers), fresh and faux florals, colourful tableware and cookware all work to add colour to your home.

CONFIDENT COLOUR You can experiment with colour in so many ways, as the examples on the opposite page show. Using colour on walls and woodwork and through artwork can imbue spaces with a joyful effervescence that brings a room to life. Gain confidence in adding colour by starting with accessories, such as a patterned lampshade or cushion, or by painting an accent chair in a bold colour.

Samuel
Benjamin
Sebastien

Finding Your Colour Scheme

Formerly of Farrow & Ball and with a decade spent as a mental health nurse, colour consultant **Victoria Hodgetts** is passionate about the impact of colour on mental well-being.

What do you love about working with colour? I absolutely adore it; it's transformative, magical even. As it's accessible to almost everyone, you don't need a huge budget to transform your home. When I work with a client, I love discovering the person behind the home and understanding their story.

Favourite colours to work with? My personal favourites are earthy shades, typically offset with a soft black for depth and definition. I love the sense of renewal and calm achieved through gentle greens and sustaining brown, while burnt ochres and verdant olives are my go-tos for an evocative and immersive scheme. There will always be a special place in my heart for pink, too; with its distinct ability to evoke different moods, it brings a transformative quality to the space, subtly shifting from peaceful to passionate.

What influences your colour choices? I love fashion and this inspires many of my colour designs; this could be high fashion, but just as often it's a stranger's outfit on the street. I'm also passionate about individual art and sculpture. I often suggest that clients use their own artwork as colour inspiration for their scheme. Nature is also a huge influence; I love how colours relate to one another in nature – there is never a 'bad' combination.

Can different colours affect how we feel? Colour intrinsically alters emotions, our responses and our subsequent behaviours. Some colours do have a universal meaning, but there can be polarity in the perception of a hue; warm spectrum colours, such as red, orange and yellow, can evoke feelings of security and comfort, but can also reflect emotions of anger and hostility. Cool spectrum colours, meanwhile, such as blue, purple and green, can be described as calm, but may also be associated with sadness or indifference.

Is a cohesive colour palette important in our homes? I think it is, but I believe this can be achieved in many different ways. It doesn't have to restrict your ability to create a diverse design. Try wherever possible to roughly map out your house scheme from the start. Budget is often a constraining factor, but having an idea in mind really helps the curation of cohesion and flow.

What rules of thumb do you adhere to when using colour? Take the 60:30:10 approach to colour application. This rule refers to the recommended distribution of colours in an interior scheme to make it visually appealing and balanced; 60 per cent of a room's colour in a dominant hue, 30 per cent in a secondary colour, and 10 per cent in an accent colour. No colour combinations are forbidden! Where schemes tend to fail is typically not in the combination itself, but rather the relative proportions of each hue.

Top tips for using colour?

- Test paint samples on large pieces of lining paper as these can be moved around the room as required.
- Rooms with low light levels love dark and strong colours, even if this does feel counterintuitive.
- White is the worst colour for small, dark rooms; it highlights all the shadows, making it feel even smaller, darker and more lifeless.
- Include neutrals, even in the boldest of schemes; a harmonious neutral creates some 'breathing space'.

DETAILED DESIGN Tongue-and-groove panelling from The English Panelling Company, painted in Farrow & Ball's 'Lamp Room Gray' complements blue Shaker style kitchen cabinets, while a shelf wrapped in marble-effect vinyl is elevated with a brass rail from the House of Brass and brackets from Corston Architectural Detail.

A Modern Vintage Palette

Experimenting with colour in my home has been quite the journey, a thrilling one at times, but also one filled with mishaps and mistakes along the way. I believe we must make errors of judgement, however, in order to uncover what we truly love, and it feels pretty special when we finally get it right.

Colour is subjective and an incredibly personal choice in our homes; a shade that works wonderfully for one individual might feel completely at odds for another. This is dependent on many factors: the aspect of a room, how much natural light it receives, how the colour makes you feel, what furniture and accessories have been used – the list is endless. That said, there are certain colours and colour combinations that I come back to time and again as they work so well together. They have also proved incredibly popular with followers on my social media channels, who ask me daily what the paint colours in my home are. Here are some of my favourite colour combinations, where I've used them, and which paint colours they are, should you want to try them for yourself:

Blue and Green

A harmonious colour pairing that reflects both coastal and country locations. I use variations of blue and green but try to keep the tones similar, so they don't create dissonance across the different spaces. The **kitchen and dining room** are painted in Farrow & Ball's 'Lamp Room Gray', a soft and timeless blue-grey which can look green in some lights. In the **bathroom** is Farrow & Ball's 'Studio Green', a rich, deep green which works particularly well with brass accents. The **living room** is painted in Benjamin Moore's 'Hamilton Blue', a timeless dark blue with green undertones; it feels very cosy in this darker space in my home that doesn't get much natural light.

Blue and Red

I use this colour combination consistently throughout my home, blue being the dominant colour and red the accent colour used across accessories, such as cushions, bedspreads or artwork. You can see this pairing in my **living room**, on my **kitchen shelves**, in the **guest bedroom**, and even in my little reading chair in the library area.

Pink and Red

I love pink and red together as they contrast so markedly but have the same undertone, which makes for an interesting pairing. I've used this combination in the **primary bedroom** of our home, where Farrow & Ball's 'Setting Plaster' sets a calm, feminine tone, while red accents sneak in from cushions, bedspreads and artwork to add a gutsy richness to the space.

Neutrals

I've used a few neutral colours to add breathing space throughout my home: Farrow & Ball's 'Shadow White' (kitchen woodwork), 'James White' (boys' bedroom) and 'Strong White' (hallway).

Other colour combinations that I love to see used include green and pink, blue and yellow, red and ochre, and terracotta and red. You can see some of these wonderfully vibrant colour pairings in *Part Three – Homes to Inspire, pages 84–219*.

BOLD & BRIGHT An unexpected blend of colours creates a distinctive and individual aesthetic in the room opposite; here, fruity pink walls blend with mustard and navy tones, which are woven in through the use of fabrics and soft furnishings. The colour scheme, though bold and bright, is limited to three to four colours to maintain a cohesive ensemble.

The Power of Nostalgia

The emotional potency of nostalgic decor in our homes is not inconsequential; a wistful nod to times gone by, these are evocative pieces that stir up happy memories and envelop us in a familiar comfort blanket.

A friend once asked me what the story was behind my ever-growing collection of vintage sailing boats, the latest addition of which is a substantial-sized beauty with elegant, though discernibly aged and slightly mottled, sails. It stands on the mantelpiece in the boys' bedroom, inviting the attention of anyone who passes by. Over the years, long-suffering ornaments, trinkets and other less noteworthy items have been hastily nudged aside to make room for my latest nautical acquisition, mostly found in flea markets or on Facebook Marketplace. I could have explained away the sailing boat obsession with a breezy 'Oh, because they look pretty', and there would be an ample dose of accuracy in my answer. In truth, however, my real love of sailing boats goes back to hazy summer days as a child spent playing at a little harbour close to where my grandparents lived on the Hampshire coast.

The horizon would be filled as far as the eye could see with boats and yachts of all shapes and sizes; something about the sea, its implied freedom and the playfulness of the sailing boats captured me then, as it does now. Memories of that characterful little harbour and its array of colourful boats embody those happy, carefree days. So, my model sailing boats may look pretty, but the sense of nostalgia they exude conjures up something much more powerful for me: joy, comfort and peace.

WHIMSICAL DECOR Nostalgia has influenced the design of much of my home, including the bedroom of my youngest sons (opposite), where a sailing boat from Facebook Marketplace infuses the space with a sense of whimsy and creates a focal point against striped, sage-green wallpaper ('Sam' from Sandberg Wallpaper). A bright throw in the bedroom of Holly Hardy's daughter echoes the colourful artwork on the walls (right). (See more of Holly's home on pages 86–103.)

Including items such as vintage bedspreads, old furniture and memorabilia in our decor can elicit a nurturing sense of familiarity, allowing us to forge a deep-rooted connection to our homes. When we buy something new, that feeling of novelty brings us fleeting moments of excitement, but nostalgia is far more powerful and is one of the most compelling ways in which we can create more authentic interiors that better reflect our sense of identity.

Grandmillennia & the Rise of 'Granny Chic'

There has been a new wave of enthusiasm for decor of yesteryear, its growing popularity fuelled by a craving for more connected, visceral spaces that support our emotional well-being. Using nostalgia in the home is not a new design concept, as our grandparents have been doing it for years, but the increasing prevalence of 'granny chic' or 'grandmillennia' in design schemes and home furnishings indicates an auspicious future for a nostalgia-based approach to interior design.

The term 'grandmillennia' – a fusion of the words grandmother and millennial – was first coined to describe an interior style that blends different eras to create an eclectic style. It has been popularized by those who have an affinity for traditional decor but also enjoy adding a contemporary twist. Nostalgia-infused wallpapers, ruffled fabrics, furniture skirts, chintz and chinoiserie are key elements of granny chic, but whether you are game for a ruffle or not, the essence of what this style of interior design represents is a home that feels evocative of times gone by; it's layered, cosy and a little sentimental.

Five Ways to Create Grandmillennial Style

1 *Pattern* – choose floral, chintzy or heritage designs across cushions, crockery and bedspreads.

2 *Wallpaper* – add a subtle floral design or go bold with a William Morris print.

3 *Furniture skirts* – cover up unsightly appliances such as a washing machine or dishwasher with a floral fabric, or use on a bathroom vanity.

4 *Fringes and ruffles* – add a ruffled cushion, fringed accent chair, pleated curtains or a bed valance.

5 *Layer upon layer* – create depth and interest by layering patterns on top of or adjacent to each other.

PATTERN PLAY Traditional design has been given a modern twist by combining Charlotte Gaisford's 'Elizabeth Blue' wallpaper with pom-pom trimmed curtains to create an eclectic aesthetic with a hint of sentimentality (opposite). (See page 180 to discover more about Charlotte and her approach to interiors.) In the guest room of my home (left), Sandberg Wallpaper's 'Karolina Blue' is paired with a red-and-white striped, ruffled bolster cushion.

Sourcing Vintage – Come Antiquing With Me

Ask me my favourite way to spend a Sunday morning, and aside from eating a leisurely breakfast of delicious pastries and coffee, I will not hesitate to tell you that a good nose around my favourite antiques store is hard to beat. The smell of musty old books, the feel of gnarled and knotty wooden furniture, a vintage French metal sign catching my eye – all at once awakening my senses and sparking interest. It is a joy to wander around and in between jumbles and piles of stuff, expectant and a little excited, because you never quite know what you might chance upon.

Sometimes I visit with a sense of regimented purpose and a requirement to fulfil: I need a chest of drawers for the boys' bedroom or I want to find a new side table perhaps. Then there are other times when I go with a completely open mind, a limited budget and not quite knowing what I may find. I rarely come out of the antiques store with what I expected to, but that's half the joy of antiquing; it's unpredictable, surprising and more than a little thrilling.

I've been antiquing for many years now and have undoubtedly picked up a few tips along the way for finding and snagging that elusive vintage gem, which I share with you here, but the real joy in antiques shopping is to be found in the experience itself.

Top Tips for Antiquing

1 *Set a budget* – decide the maximum amount you want to spend and stick to it: antiquing can be budget-friendly but can also quickly become expensive if you allow it to!

2 *Research your item* – if you know what you're looking for, do a little research first to get a rough estimate of what you should be paying for it.

3 *Be prepared to barter* – you have nothing to lose by offering a lower price; most dealers will expect you to do this anyway and have factored this into the price. You can usually expect to get 10–15 per cent off the asking price.

4 *Go with your gut* – if it feels like the right piece, at the right price, be decisive because it may not be there the next day.

5 *Have fun* – enjoy the experience and don't be disappointed if you come away with nothing. Just save your money for the next trip.

ANTIQUE HUNTING Much of the decor in my home has been sourced through thrifting at antiques stores, secondhand shops and flea markets. From old chairs to vintage fabrics and larger pieces like cabinets and cupboards, there is a plethora of treasures waiting to be found. My top tips include setting a budget, researching pieces of interest and having the confidence to barter.

The Versatility of Secondhand

There is something wonderfully versatile about older furniture, many pieces of which you can pick up inexpensively from online secondhand sites such as Facebook Marketplace and eBay. Or if you have a slightly bigger budget and specific pieces in mind, Vinterior and Pamono can be wonderful sources of antique furniture. For me, these pieces will almost always trump mass-produced, off-the-shelf items, which can lack originality and whose function is predetermined and often limited. Add to that the quality of craftsmanship and the character that older pieces bring to a space, along with the environmental benefits of repurposing secondhand furniture, and they can be hard to beat.

Over the years, I've picked up a plethora of second-hand pieces for my home, including vintage Thonet bar-stools for my kitchen, an old Victorian dining table, and a beautiful pitch-pine chest of drawers, to mention just a few. But one of my favourite finds is a distinctly timeworn £40 wooden cupboard; it's not a valuable antique but a simple piece which has been useful in a multitude of spaces within my home, proving its versatility in more ways than one. It is currently a bedside table (nightstand), adding a charming warmth to the guest room, but has also been used as a bathroom cabinet, hiding all those unsightly bathroom bits and pieces, as well as a handy little side table, perfect for a lamp and a book or two.

My Top Tips for Buying Secondhand Online

1 *Set up alerts/notifications* – do this for items you're searching for, so you never miss out.

2 *Watch for woodworm* – if you're buying old wooden furniture, check for woodworm and ask if it has been treated for this.

3 *Research useful search words* – for example, when looking for an old dining table, I might use a variety of the following: 'vintage table', 'farmhouse table' 'Victorian dining table' and 'rustic French table'.

CONSCIOUS DECORATING Antique or secondhand furniture, like the treasured pieces shown opposite in the home of Helen May Petschel (see more on page 192), exude craftsmanship and character, while imbuing spaces with an unrivalled originality and charm. Repurposing older pieces can also be a more environmentally conscious way of decorating your home than buying mass-produced, off-the-shelf items.

oiseless

The Future is Vintage

'Out with the new, in with the old' is the mantra of **Lucy Ward**, Vice President of Vinterior. An online platform, it brings together vintage and antique sellers from around the world, with a focus on allowing people to access one-of-a-kind pieces while also being kinder to the planet.

What is the ethos behind Vinterior? Vinterior is a design-led, circular marketplace on a mission to change the future of the furniture industry by making it frictionless to buy and sell preloved pieces, which are inherently more sustainable.

Has the popularity and demand for secondhand pieces increased? When Vinterior launched in 2016, Sandrine Zhang Ferron, our founder, was told it was niche to only be working with secondhand products. Fast-forward almost a decade and the tide has changed; while there's still a way to go, people have a better understanding of the benefits of buying secondhand. With many quality preowned pieces increasing in value over time, shoppers know it represents a good investment over new furniture that depreciates immediately and is less durable.

What are the environmental benefits of buying secondhand? With over 22 million pieces of furniture going into landfill every year, something has to change, so repurposing furniture or buying secondhand is a lot kinder to the planet, with zero carbon emissions from manufacturing and production.

How do vintage and secondhand pieces add character to a home? Older, quality pieces are a shortcut to creating an individual home that doesn't look anything like the neighbours' mass-produced, identikit living room. Homeowners have a real desire to build characterful spaces that represent their personalities – they don't want their houses to look like everyone else's. Having said that, secondhand doesn't need to be old; since opening up the platform to individual sellers we are seeing more quality, contemporary products being circulated through Vinterior. It's great to be able to cater for all tastes and get more people away from buying brand-new items.

What are the top five items bought on Vinterior?

- Mid-century sideboard
- Bobbin-style furniture and barley twist pieces, along with other Edwardian pieces from the early 1900s
- Togo and Mario Bellini soft and oversized seating
- Staffordshire ceramic dogs
- Murano glassware lighting

Best thing about buying vintage? I love the patina that vintage furniture acquires over time. That's something you simply can't replicate.

Top tips for sourcing vintage online? Always measure your space (and your front door!). Use Vinterior's 'saved search' function to be the first to be alerted by email when relevant pieces land. Look for named designers, which can be great for initial purchases if you don't feel as familiar with the product and want to ensure the piece will be reliable. For example, Robin Day is a great place to start for British mid-20th century modern design, or G-Plan who were masters at creating affordable furniture using high-quality materials.

PRELOVED PIECES Online marketplaces, including Vinterior and Pamono, continue to grow in popularity due to the vast range of preowned and antique pieces they offer from sellers around the world. From secondhand dining chairs to design-led collectables, finding one-of-a-kind, sustainable pieces that add individuality to a space has never been easier.

PART TWO
Rooms to Inspire

The Kitchen

Profound memories and moments of exquisitely simple pleasure are often synonymous with the kitchen: chaotic cake-baking with children, conversations with friends who linger over a hot drink, and where effortless contentment can be found during a slow Sunday morning filled with an indulgent breakfast and strong coffee. Nostalgia and sentimentality aside, the connection between food and comfort is a basic but powerful one, and so, where better to harness that sense of sustenance and joie de vivre than in the kitchen?

Creating a Sense of Self in the Hub of Your Home

There is no other space that encapsulates me more than my kitchen. I have vintage French poster prints on the shelves (a nostalgic reminder of trips to Paris as a twentysomething), little Breton bowls embellished with my children's names, and memorabilia from family holidays. Every corner has been filled with curios and cookware collected over many years: pots, plates and utensils that bring genuine joy every time they are used. It is neither coincidence nor a happy accident that the kitchen is the most personal, and arguably the most curated, space in my home, but rather an intentional design choice to create a specific *feeling*. I wanted more than anything when decorating the kitchen to suffuse the space with individuality and a sense of identity, and to be enveloped by the little pieces that make up the nuances of myself.

The dream kitchen quite often remains just that, a dream, a vision or a saved Pinterest picture. We are forever striving to make this hard-working space the ultimate in everything: practical, functional and aesthetically pleasing, to say the least, but sometimes we must work with the space we have. Making every corner count and sparking interest where ordinarily it might not exist is a powerful way to transform the kitchen into a place of charm and character and one that is completely individual to you.

ALL IN THE DETAIL I've filled every available shelf, corner and wall in my kitchen with a cluster of curios that hold meaning and add personality to this functional space. A collection of my favourite ceramics (right) includes a 1950s Hungarian decorative plate that I sourced on Etsy. Original bistro-style bar-stools add a vintage element (opposite).

en
Poudre
Soluble
FLOUR

A French Bistro-Inspired Space

Art Deco-inspired globe pendant lights cast a lustrous glow above intimate wooden tables, around which curved Thonet chairs are clustered together. A backdrop of vintage French posters elicits a sense of faded glamour, while the intoxicating aroma of fresh pastries and coffee pervades the air. The classic scene of a Parisian bistro or café evokes elegant, yet casual dining, timeless decor and 19th-century French charm: a blueprint that works incredibly well when designing a modern vintage kitchen. It maximizes the aesthetic impact and yet feels bulletproof against the fading appeal of passing trends.

The vibrant milieu of chic Parisian cafés first captivated me on a trip to Paris aged 21; such was its effect on me that what followed was many years of mood boarding, sketching and daydreaming about creating my own French-inspired bistro kitchen. It would be some 15 years later, however, before I was able to harness the inspiration I'd held on to so ardently and implement it in the design of our own kitchen.

Capturing the essence of a bustling French café filled with conversation, lingering meals and elegant decor requires placing the emphasis on both atmosphere and design elements in order to create a cohesive, yet practical aesthetic. Implementing even just a few of the decorating and styling ideas outlined in the following tips in your kitchen will allow you to create the timeless and classic ambience of a French bistro.

Top Tips for Creating a Café-style Kitchen:

1 *Bistro chairs* – iconic Thonet bentwood café chairs and bar-stools are synonymous with Parisian bistros.

2 *Art Deco-inspired lighting* – large globe pendant lights combined with more intimate wall sconces add a warm and intimate ambience, reminiscent of a cosy corner in a French brasserie.

3 *French bistro table* – a small, round, oval or square table with a marble or wooden top and decorative iron pedestal makes for an elegant dining option (and is an ideal space-saver for smaller kitchens).

4 *Vintage French poster prints* – include decorative poster prints, such as those by Alphonse Mucha, famous for his colourful and stylized advertisements during the Art Nouveau period in Paris.

5 *Metro/subway tiles or wooden panelling* – create texture and add interest to the walls in classic bistro style.

FRENCH-INSPIRED KITCHEN Café-style bistro chairs in the kitchen of this London Edwardian property belonging to creative designer Roxanne Fregona and photographer Chris Pugh create an informal, yet elegant ambience in a traditional, galley-shaped kitchen, while offering a practical, yet pretty, space-saving seating solution (opposite and right).

Balancing Practicality with Aesthetics

Designing and decorating a kitchen can often feel akin to walking a tightrope: the overwhelm of trying to achieve a sensible balance of practicality with a space that looks good can be profound. The hard-working kitchen is usually where the majority of our time is spent and is normally the most expensive and permanent room we install. Therefore, creating a space that is both practical and a joy to be in is vital. That's a lot to get right.

Many designers will tell you that functionality is essential in the kitchen, which of course it largely is, but it need not be the overriding factor when planning and curating this space. Indeed, there are many who believe you should create a kitchen where the emphasis is on personality. Combining both in some way is more than achievable, and with some imaginative decoration you can have a space that is both pretty and practical.

Ideas for Practical Style

1 *Utility sink skirt* – cover any unsightly appliances with a fabric utility skirt for a soft silhouette and an opportunity to add pattern and colour.

2 *Install a pan rack or rail* – save your cupboard space for less attractive cookware and hang pots and pans from a pan rack, suspended from the ceiling, or a pan rail attached to the wall.

3 *Shelves versus cupboards* – open shelving is an easy way to add interest and personality, but if you can't bear to be parted from your cupboards or need extra storage, consider removing the fronts and displaying your favourite crockery and cookware here.

PRACTICAL & PRETTY Decorative plates displayed on the walls of Olive and Hugo Guest's colourful kitchen add warmth and character (right). A collection of copper pots on a handy pan rack create an eye-catching focal point in the home of Christen Pears, while saving precious drawer space (opposite).

4 *Kitchen island/prep table* – islands and prep tables are a great way to add depth and interest to a kitchen, while providing extra workspace; use a kitchen trolley or mobile butcher's block if you're short on space, or, alternatively, include a vintage prep table that doubles as a dining space.

5 *Display utensils, plates, cookbooks and art* – create a kitchen with warmth and personality by displaying items that represent you, such as ceramics collected on holiday, favourite cookbooks or a piece of art you love, and save drawer space by arranging wooden utensils in pretty pots or hanging them on a utensil rail.

A Modern-Day Pantry for Any Space

The allure of a modern-day pantry, which offers the promise of elevated organization opportunities combined with a space that embodies charm and nostalgia, is hard to resist. Curating a space that includes aesthetically pleasing shelves lined with orderly jars of cooking staples, herbs and spices, and even small appliances, offers a solution to achieving a streamlined, clutter-free kitchen (surely, one of life's greatest luxuries).

Often associated with beautiful old Victorian kitchens where the original 'butler's pantry' was used for storage, pantries are the perfect place to go vintage; reclaimed wooden shelves, traditional brass hardware, and antique cookware, pots or utensils work together to create a beautiful, yet functional kitchen space.

However, if you're reading this and thinking, a pantry sounds like a dream but I don't have a walk-in space or area large enough to include such a luxury in the kitchen, then you are not alone, and I, for one, shared such a dilemma. Having long fantasized about how I could conjure up an extra room for a walk-in pantry or squeeze in a vintage freestanding cupboard somewhere, reality hit home, and I had to rethink my thwarted pantry plans. Maximizing every nook and cranny of my kitchen to create a practical, yet beautiful space was the ultimate goal, so earmarking an area that could become a 'pantry' corner became the obvious solution. Vintage in style, while blending in with the rest of my kitchen decor, it would be a space that simultaneously ticked some practical boxes too.

Having proved to be one of the most popular areas of my home on social media, the pantry corner in my kitchen was relatively easy and budget-friendly to create. Below I've listed some top tips for creating your own space-saving alternative to the much-coveted pantry. However, if you are lucky enough to have a walk-in space or freestanding cupboard, then you could also apply these ideas to that area.

Top Tips for Creating a Pantry Corner

1 *Purpose* – firstly, decide how your pantry will be used – for example, perhaps as a coffee station or to house food and baking ingredients.

2 *Panelling* – include some tongue-and-groove panelling to add a traditional feel to the space, while adding depth and interest.

3 *Shelving* – choose a style in keeping with the rest of your kitchen decor for a cohesive fit and include as many shelves as the space will allow for maximum storage, or, alternatively, keep the space simple with just one or two shelves.

4 *Storage jars/baskets* – decant food and baking ingredients into vintage vessels such as Kilner jars and store vegetables in wicker baskets for aesthetically pleasing and easily accessible storage.

5 *Brass rail* – adding a rail can really elevate shelves and give them a high-end appearance.

IMAGINATIVE DESIGN A spare nook in Anita Russell's modest cottage kitchen has been transformed into a diminutive, yet practical pantry, with tongue-and-groove panelling for added depth and interest and traditional shelves for displaying food staples. Making every inch of this quaint corner count, a handy brass rail provides functional and aesthetically pleasing storage for crockery.

The Dining Room

When we look beyond the perceived conventions and functionality of a space, such as the unassuming dining room, we can begin creating spaces that transcend the norm and feel elevated, distinctive and even remarkable.

Reimagining Your Dining Room

Reinventing a room by redefining zones within that space not only breathes fresh life into interiors but also carves out areas that have the potential for a myriad of different roles, while answering the demands of its occupants. Due to our ever-increasing needs and requirements, our homes are no longer just a place to rest, eat and sleep; spaces must also be conducive to productivity and work, and offer respite from the chaos of the world around us. Rooms once intended for a single purpose, such as the dining room traditionally used as a place to gather formally for mealtimes, are finding new lives as studies and offices, or merely as a space to retreat from the hustle and bustle of life.

Decorating the dining room often ceases once the table and chairs are in place, leaving a chasm of untapped promise in this humble space. Over the next few pages, you'll find inspiration for transforming a dining room from practical and perfunctory to a space that meets workable and aesthetic expectations. There are also ideas for infusing the room with abundant character.

DISTINCTIVE DINING Individuality is at the heart of the dining space (below), with bold, hand-painted stripes creating a striking background to a collection of curios and artwork, while a large vine combined with a collection of original paintings adds ambience and drama to the dining room featured opposite.

A Room Within a Room – Creating a Whimsical Home Library

There is something rather quaint and old-worldly about sitting down to dinner in a well-stocked library – a transient feeling of being spirited away to another world or a different period of time when modern distractions cannot intrude. A beguiling space of floor-to-ceiling bookshelves that entices one in, offering cocoon-like comfort and escapism; a room within a room with cosy corners that feel safe and inviting.

When I first came up with the idea of creating a library in my previously uninspiring and undeniably soulless dining room, little did I know that millions of people across the world would have such a passionate response to the photographs and videos I shared of the project on social media, or that it would inspire so many to install their own little 'libraries'.

The very notion of owning a library, to live in a house large enough for those enchanting floor-to-ceiling bookshelves, seemed fanciful; a mere pipe dream confined to childhood and certainly not achievable in a modest semi-detached house (duplex) with little space to play with. It is all too easy to dismiss our interior visions as unobtainable, perhaps because they seem too difficult or expensive to achieve, but when we start to see our homes as sanctuaries where our aspirations can, in fact, be realized with a little imagination and innovative thinking, almost anything is possible.

A lack of space or budget would no longer become a barrier to my fantastical interior ambitions, and so began my quest to find a suitable space for my mini library. An unused wall at the back of the dining room, a space previously of little character or purpose, offered the perfect opportunity for floor-to-ceiling bookshelves. The project, which was done on a fairly tight budget, transformed the space from awkward and dull to one with layers, character and individuality, which was also supremely useful.

Books have a powerful way of elevating any interior space, particularly corners that have little in the way of interesting features or functional purpose; they can reflect our love of escapism, our literary journeys and our deepest-held aspirations. The ability to browse among books in your own library is an unparalleled cure for boredom and almost certainly an effective stress-reliever.

And, of course, we should not overlook the sensory connection we have with books; there is nothing quite like turning the pages of an engrossing novel, leafing through an old childhood text, a musty but curiously comforting smell emanating from its well-thumbed pages, or enjoying blissful silence while our eyes roam luxuriously over the beautifully curated pages of a favourite interiors book.

BEGUILING BOOKSHELVES Building a library in the dining area of my home transformed the space from characterless to cosy and comforting. Painted in Farrow & Ball's 'Treron', the bookshelves complement the grey-green tones of Farrow & Ball's 'Lamp Room Gray' on the adjoining walls. A brass rail from House of Brass and secondhand vintage ladder add a whimsical touch to the library.

Styling the Dining Area

Whether an open-plan kitchen/dining area in a new build or a separate room in a period property, spacious or small, there is ample opportunity to foster an ambience individual to the self-effacing dining room. A statement piece of art, a characterful vintage table with quirky dining chairs, or a head-turning pendant light can all work to lavish this often overlooked room with an air of character and charm.

Artfully arranged furniture, along with a little judicious styling, can allow even the smallest of dining rooms to accommodate sufficient pieces to create a cosy effect. It is amazing how much more spacious a room feels when self-contained areas are established on its periphery – a dining table takes centre stage, flanked by a cosy reading corner, while height is manipulated through the shrewd use of built-in cupboards or shelves, for example. Create corners that invite the eye to linger awhile: a sideboard displaying antique tableware or glassware, perhaps a collection of art prints, or a vintage vase with an arrangement of seasonal foliage.

Top Tips for Styling a Modern Vintage Dining Room

1 *Dining table* – a sturdy wooden table with statement dining chairs will anchor the space and add warmth.

2 *Artwork* – a large piece of artwork or a poster print can create a colourful focal point.

3 *Storage* – built-in shelves or a vintage cupboard for displaying antique linens or tableware will help layer the space and add interest.

4 *Lighting* – a rise-and-fall pendant light over the dining table will create adaptable ambience.

5 *Floral display* – mix faux and fresh flowers for a vibrant, colourful centrepiece.

LAYERED INTEREST An antique dresser in the dining room (opposite top right) creates useful storage for tableware and crockery, while adding an additional layer to the space and drawing the eye around the room. Artworks and decorative accessories help to elevate a dining space from merely functional to interesting and individual (right and opposite).

THE BEDROOM

Stepping inside the bedroom is, at times, to avail oneself of a quiet interlude away from the maelstrom of life; this is no place for work, chores or preoccupation but a secure haven among the other spaces in our home, set aside for rest and repose.

An infinitely personal space, the bedroom is a sanctuary for indulging our innermost creativity, however that might manifest itself, whether it be through the colour we paint the walls, the kind of artwork we display or the furniture we layer the space with. The pieces that surround you from first thing in the morning until you drop off to sleep at night are remarkably significant; the sum of their collective benefits helps to create a deeply individual space conducive to restorative comfort.

Unbound by the responsibilities that circumscribe the design of hard-working spaces such as the kitchen and dining room, the bedroom instead offers an exciting opportunity to relax the reins a little and have fun with colour and pattern. This design dispensation should, of course, be balanced with the imperative need for a calm and cosy retreat; there is a plethora of ways to interpret that brief depending on your own personal taste and preferences, and a little experimentation to discover what will work best for you is always worthwhile in the long run.

Curatorial magic can make any room come alive, but when executed authentically in the bedroom, the effect is an intentional cacophony of styles, fabrics and colours that creates the most wonderfully individual space. Bedrooms are without a doubt the spaces that excite me the most when designing an interior scheme.

EXPLORE CREATIVITY A miscellany of colour and pattern defines the aesthetics of the bedroom (opposite), with the wallpaper 'London Birds' by Charlotte Gaisford dominating the design scheme. A collection of original art is central to the decor of interior designer Lloyd Hodgkinson's bedroom (right) and is complemented with a patterned headboard and vibrant bedding to create a truly individual space. (See page 208 to learn more about Lloyd's colourful home.)

21st-Century Romantic

Oscillating somewhere between the enchanting bedroom of a French château and that of an eccentric English country house was the sweet spot in which I envisaged the interior of our primary bedroom to sit. An amalgamation of favoured design styles, combining antique furniture, romantic lighting and gloriously fanciful fabrics, would make up the layers of a space whose prerequisites, although not extensive, were non-negotiable: a colourful bedroom that felt both individual and peaceful.

At its core, the bedroom feels timeless and traditional; period features, including a Victorian-style brass bed and fireplace, are contrasted with the softness of linen bedding, vintage bedspreads and cushions, with original oil paintings adding an artistic flourish. A subtle femininity, emanating from the muted plaster-pink walls, an antique occasional chair and delicate brass elements, is tempered by the simplicity of a vintage pitch-pine chest of drawers and bedside tables (nightstands) boasting a rich and authoritative patina.

Peppering the space with contemporary elements, such as a modern lampshade, mirror or candlesticks, creates a multidimensional aesthetic that avoids being too contrived or overly quaint. Buffering the design scheme against frivolity by minimizing the use of both old and new ensures a harmonious balance between the two. Here, I provide some inspirational ideas for creating a modern romantic bedroom style, which could also be incorporated into a variety of bedroom design schemes.

Top Tips for Creating a Modern Romantic Bedroom

1 *Chandelier* – a statement light fitting such as a vintage-style chandelier adds both romance and a feeling of whimsy.

2 *The bed* – choose from a traditional, Victorian-style brass bed or a box-spring bed with a pretty valance and patterned headboard, or for a touch of drama, install a four-poster bed frame.

3 *Colour* – romantic and relaxing hues such as muted pink, sage green or faded lilac are great colour choices for the bedroom; and for the ultimate in cosy and cocooning, colour-drench the ceilings and woodwork in the same colour as the walls.

4 *Soft, layered fabrics* – relaxed bedding in linen or brushed cotton adds softness to the space, especially when layered with a vintage bedspread or eiderdown, and can be complemented with long, luxurious curtains and a textured or patterned rug.

5 *Vintage florals* – add framed botanical prints, such as those by painter Pierre-Joseph Redouté, or an antique oil painting for added colour and interest.

UNDERSTATED ELEGANCE Vintage linens in a glazed cupboard add a romantic undertone to the bedroom of retired homewares dealer Helen May Petschel, while a simply patterned curtain softly frames the window. Antique furniture and a French-style bedstead add an understated charm to this bedroom (opposite). Pastel-coloured twisted candles echo the plaster pink walls in my bedroom, while a wooden bobbin lamp base from Laura Ashley adds texture to the space (overleaf).

The Importance of Good Bedding

The impact of a well-dressed bed on both the aesthetics of a bedroom and the quality of sleep enjoyed there should never be underestimated. Bed linen, blankets and bedspreads can transform a room, for better or worse, either elevating it to layered and interesting or, conversely, creating a vacuous space with little to no personality that feels disjointed from the decor of the rest of the room.

The bed you choose, along with the mattress and bedding you clothe it with, are collectively the most important and long-lasting investment you can make for the bedroom. Setting the tone for the room, the colour, style and fabric of the bedding can dramatically alter the mood and atmosphere of the space, and there really is no substitute for quality bedding when it comes to maximizing a decent night's sleep.

Adding a variety of textures to the bed in the same family of tones can create a warm and layered ambience; bed linen in relaxed, muted colours can be complemented with a patterned bedspread or quilt and accessorized with cushions, either plain or in a different pattern. The finished look is an imaginative bedroom interior enriched with colour, fabrics and texture. A simpler, pared-back bed with a more neutral colour palette can, of course, also be cosy and inviting, but be wary of an all-white scheme, which can create a nondescript aesthetic that overwhelms the room.

Choosing which material to use for your bedding can be overwhelming, or maybe it is something you have simply never considered before. A few years ago, I swapped my standard cotton bedding for linen and bamboo, and it had a remarkable impact on the quality of my sleep – for the better. Below are some of my favourite types of bedding, a list worth considering if you are looking to elevate your bed linen.

My Top Four Types of Bedding

1 *Linen* – relaxed look, gets softer with each wash, lasts for years if well looked after, good for body temperature control.

2 *Bamboo* – environmentally friendly, super soft and also breathable.

3 *Egyptian cotton* – creates a luxurious look due to its smooth finish and excellent quality, and also very soft, durable and breathable.

4 *Brushed cotton* – a soft and fluffy texture, feels cosy and comforting, especially in the cooler months.

BEDDING STYLE Enhance the aesthetics of the bedroom with a well-dressed bed that blends comfort and style, such as those featured opposite. Relaxed linens (top left) soften spaces and help control body temperature, while a vibrant bedspread and layered patterns, as featured in textile designer Charlotte Gaisford's guest bedroom (top right), can add instant character. The cushion fabric bottom right is by Mark Hearld.

The Living Room

A certain kind of magic emanates from a living space that is enriched with intrigue – a charm woven into every nook or cranny through a carefully curated blend of old and new. Pieces with a story to tell jostle for attention alongside their more contemporary counterparts, while curios and colourful artwork create a punchy backdrop, and comforting sofas and armchairs ground the space. The modern vintage living room is full of life, vibrancy and charm, but its design is also considered and relaxed.

COLOURFUL COMFORT Vibrant pink walls painted in Farrow & Ball's 'Fruit Fool' create an energetic feeling in the living room of Holly Hardy (see also page 86), which has been tempered with neutral-coloured sofas and a simple jute rug. A collection of colourful paintings, sourced mainly through online auctions adds balance to the colour scheme (opposite and above).

MY FAMILY AND
OTHER SEEDLINGS
LALAGE SNOW
BRIAN POLCYN with
MICHAEL RUHLMAN
PÂTÉ, CONFIT, RILLETTE
HENRI MATISSE
TASCHEN

Contemporary Meets Traditional

Be it big or small, situated within a grand period property or a modest apartment, the living room should spark interest, entice us in and extend an invitation to put up one's feet and stay awhile. Curating a living space that embodies a timeless quality, with comfort at the forefront of the design, creates an aesthetic synonymous with individuality and longevity, while feeling intrinsically authentic.

Dovetailing older pieces with more contemporary elements in the living room breathes life into the space, evoking charm and interest, while enveloping us in a space we are loathe to leave. Vintage or antique decor nourishes our senses and holds our attention; it could be the worn patina of an old sideboard or console table that catches our eye, a comfy and inviting secondhand armchair coaxing us to rest and relax, or perhaps a colourful art collection that diverts us in a welcome moment of distraction.

We spend a considerable amount of time in our living room, so it needs to be enjoyed effortlessly and over a sustained period. Including older pieces in the decor is the antithesis of off-the-shelf purchases with their habitually short-lived appeal; antiques' immunity to the ebb and flow of passing trends gives them an indefinite charm and a feeling of dependable permanence, which doesn't fade easily over time. This makes vintage pieces a wise investment for any living room, and they are especially advantageous for those who don't have the time, inclination or budget to change their interior too often.

Above all else, the living room, in a similar way to the bedroom, should reflect our individuality and be a space in which we feel altogether at ease; comfort in this room is paramount.

AUTHENTIC DESIGN Antiques and contemporary accessories are artfully blended to create individuality in the living room of hoteliers Olive and Hugo Guest (opposite), including a secondhand chair reupholstered in an Ian Mankin fabric and a lampshade by Matthew Williamson for Pooky Lighting. Farrow & Ball's 'Fake Tan' on the panelled walls creates a colourful, yet muted backdrop for a selection of artwork and trinkets (opposite and see also page 120). Artwork sourced from online marketplace Selency adds interest above this mantelpiece (right).

Curating Creativity & Cohesion

Harnessing a unified colour palette, ensuring a moderate blend of classic and contemporary, and balancing the right amount of furniture sounds like a tall order for one room. And it is, but like any approach to designing an interior scheme, simplifying it as much as possible ensures an aesthetic that is considered and carefully contemplated rather than one that feels overdesigned and haphazard.

The design for my living room started quite simply with a rug. As noted in my 7-step formula for creating a cohesive design scheme for modern vintage decor (see pages 12–15), taking inspiration from just one item of decor is often enough to galvanize and spearhead an interior scheme in its entirety. Picking out the two main colours from my rug, I was able to build a simple and restricted colour palette on which to base the decoration of the room, from the colour of the walls to the style and colour of the sofas, right down to the accent colour I wanted to use for the accessories and soft furnishing, such as cushions, throws and artwork. The result is an aesthetic that appears curated, yet relaxed and organic; colours, tones and furniture are all working in perfect harmony and nothing jars or feels out of place.

Layering furniture so that the eye is drawn beyond and across the room is key to creating a well-proportioned space that avoids feeling too cluttered; dainty, more elegant pieces are balanced with larger items of furniture, ensuring each piece has room to breathe. To solidify a cohesive scheme, add accessories and artwork that pick out the tones of your chosen colour palette.

While a considered design scheme across the space as a whole is key, there is one dispensation to this rule when it comes to creating instant character. The living room is a wonderful space to include an element of surprise; by adding one or two profoundly individual pieces, such as an unusual item of furniture or a piece of artwork which does not necessarily fit exactly with the rest of the interior scheme, you can lift the space and make it unreservedly unique to you.

COHESIVE CHARACTER A bold, yet restrained colour scheme creates a sense of cohesion and calm in my living room, where Benjamin Moore's 'Hamilton Blue' on the walls is teamed with red and green accents, which are woven into the scheme through accessories and artwork. A modern take on the classic Chesterfield, the addition of Sofas & Stuff's Exbury sofa in V&A's 'Flowering Kale' fabric adds pattern and texture to the space.

Adding Architectural Charm

Unadorned walls and ceilings can feel a little like a cake without any icing; the main ingredients are there but it doesn't feel quite finished. We can be so focused on the paint colours, the big pieces of furniture or the pretty cushions that we often forget about the smaller architectural details that can add some serious weight to the character and charm you bring to a space.

Older properties, often said to have 'good bones' as they have retained period features such as original cornicing, architraves and mantelpieces, ooze instant charm because these are the covetable details that give the room depth and a sense of history. However, some properties have had these features stripped away over the years, while many newer homes are constructed without any standout architectural features at all. It is entirely possible to create charm in any kind of home, regardless of its period or size, and the living room provides ample opportunity to do this.

Whether you live in a period property that has lost some of its original features, an apartment or a bungalow that doesn't have any standout details, or a new build that lacks character, here are some ideas for adding architectural charm to your home.

Five Ways to Add Architectural Detail

1 *Cornicing, ceiling roses (medallions) and architraves* – an effective way to add depth and prominence to ceilings, lighting and doorways.

2 *Mouldings and trims* – an inexpensive method of highlighting artwork and adding detail to the walls.

3 *Fireplace and mantelpiece* – reinstate a period fireplace with a reclaimed mantelpiece and insert from reclamation yards or online marketplaces, or if in a new-build property, a frame can be constructed and plastered to create a focal point in the room.

4 *Wooden beams* – a great way to add detail to the ceilings of bungalows and new builds to create a cosy cottage aesthetic.

5 *Window seat* – creates a cosy and comfortable area and allows for extra storage.

ROOM WITH A VIEW A cosy window seat crafted into the bay window of a former Georgian vicarage gives this space an additional layer of interest, while also providing an extra seating area. A vintage floor lamp has been updated with a contemporary pleated lampshade from Elizabeth Hay Design.

The Bathroom

The bathroom can be a place of quiet contemplation or a fresh and vibrant room that invigorates the senses with its playful appearance. Whichever way the design pendulum swings, creating a timeless interior that piques your imagination while fulfilling its practical function will guarantee a space that's both nurturing and joyful.

Often a somewhat perfunctory participant rather than a key player in our interiors, the bathroom serves an altogether different purpose to any other space in the home; it does not offer comfort in the way the bedroom or living room does, nor is it a place in which to gather and be sociable as with the kitchen or dining room. Its purpose is primarily defined in the moments when we begin our morning and end our evening, yet it can still play a key role in the overall aesthetic of your home, and so attention to detail here is crucial.

Creating a Timeless Bathroom

I have found that bathroom trends come and go more frequently than those for any other room, which can be a little disconcerting given this is another space that can be both costly and time-consuming to change or update. Striking a decorative balance that feels both classic and contemporary and will weather the test of time comes down to some carefully considered planning and design.

Permanent fixtures such as the bathtub, sink and tiles should be enduring pieces that you are going to love for many years to come, while more transient design elements like wall colour, artwork and freestanding bathroom furniture such as cupboards can be switched up over time if you fancy a change.

Whether you opt for a quiet, considered aesthetic combining a neutral palette with traditional decor, or veer towards a more colourful design scheme where a striking wallpaper or tile colour takes prominence, ensure your inspiration is based on longevity and what feels authentic to you rather than a passing trend that has temporarily caught your attention.

For a timeless design, look to traditional elements like a roll-top bathtub, Victorian-style sink and neutral tiles, or conversely, add tongue-and-groove panelling and pair it with a decorative wallpaper in a classic English design, such as those by William Morris, Sanderson or Colefax and Fowler.

TIMELESS DESIGN A classic claw-foot bathtub sits centre stage in the bathroom of lawyer Kasturi Wren (see also page 104), where serenity is harnessed through a monochrome colour scheme, punctuated only by burnt-orange accents from fabrics and accessories. Warmth is woven into the space through rustic elements, including a wooden table and antique chair, while artwork creates further interest.

A Space for Individuality

Owing to their smaller size and the fact we don't spend a great deal of time in them, as is the case with guest rooms or utility areas, bathrooms can be a wonderful space to push the boundaries of colour and pattern and be emphatic in expressing your individuality.

If your bathroom is on the diminutive side, lean into its bijou proportions and create a charm-filled space with a unique wallpaper from an independent design house and one or two discerning antiques. Soften the space with a fabric sink skirt around the vanity unit and add a vintage wall cabinet or antique pot cupboard to house unsightly, yet essential, accessories. A bathroom that melds practicality with idiosyncrasy, laced with a little whimsical charm, exudes a *savoir faire* that's neither stuffy nor showy, but simply poised in its understated, somewhat faded elegance.

Defy the conventions of clichéd bathroom decor and make it personal by hanging decorative plates or artwork on the walls and add books and curios to an opportune corner to create a cosy, lived-in feel. Injecting playful elements will punctuate the space with curiosity and character; a stencilled floor, vibrant rug or patterned blinds (shades) can all infuse the space with an exuberant energy that is both easy and inexpensive to achieve.

If you have the space and budget, a statement bathtub or an arched shower entrance can add real drama to a bathroom, and paired with stripy tiles or a bold wallpaper, the room will feel both exciting and joyful. As with any interior space, enthusiasm and gusto for a scheme needs to be balanced with a touch of restraint to best achieve an aesthetic that doesn't look disjointed or as though it's been thrown together in haste. Choose one or two statement pieces or design elements and allow those to take centre stage.

JOYFULLY DIFFERENT Wallpaper by Ottoline de Vries and a fabric sink skirt add touches of colourful whimsy to this bathroom (opposite top right). Blue pinstripe tiles from Your Tiles create a statement in an arched shower (opposite bottom right), while artwork set against Edward Bulmer's 'Jonquil' (opposite top left) adds interest to the same bathroom space. Natural materials and muted shades dominate Anita Russell's bathroom (right). (See page 138 to discover more about Anita's lovely home.)

Lighting & Accessories

Lighting is an essential element in bathroom design, and it needs careful consideration and planning to achieve the right balance of practicality and ambience. The lighting you choose is also influenced by and dependent on the type of space you have, whether it is small or large, for example, or if there is a natural light source or not. A warm, soft glow from elegant wall sconces creates a gentle lustre that fills the space with an affable luminosity and is more flattering than harsh, bright overhead lights. A statement pendant light can illuminate a darker space and add timeless elegance to a room that is quite often, by default, dominated by newer surfaces and decor.

Layering lighting sources by using more than one type of light fitting in different zones of the bathroom is an effective way to balance ambience with practicality. Combine a chandelier-style light that brightens the whole space with wall sconces above a bathroom vanity for a more intimate glow, or install an over-bath pendant light for a touch of luxury. Consider task lighting in areas where directional light is more useful, such as recessed downlights in a shower space or low-level floor washers activated by a motion sensor, which can be incredibly helpful when navigating the space at night.

Top Tips for Choosing Bathroom Lighting

1 *Check the IP rating* – consider where each light fitting will be located, as it will require an appropriate IP rating depending on the light's proximity to the room's waterworks.

2 *Layer lighting sources* – split the bathroom into zones and include a lighting source for each area, such as the shower, bathtub and vanity sink.

3 *Fit dimmers and use warm-white bulbs* – to create atmosphere and for a favourable light that softens the space.

4 *Pair the lighting with the type of bathroom* – a shared or family bathroom may need lighting to suit all needs, while a smaller en-suite bathroom may benefit from softer, less intense lighting.

5 *Add a statement light* – a chandelier or patterned lampshades on wall sconces can add interest and drama for an individual and characterful bathroom.

LIGHT IT UP Elegant wall sconces, like the 'Putney' from Jim Lawrence, create a soft glow above a vanity unit and add decorative interest to the walls of my modern traditional bathroom (opposite). An industrial-style pendant light provides useful illumination in the bathroom (right), while adding a vintage feel to the space.

F. CHAMPENOIS
PARIS
F. CHAMPENOIS
ALFONS MUCHA (1898)
balanceme

FLEURS ET PLANTES
CAPE TOWN
LOUIS
NORMAN GRANZ
PRESENTS AN
EVENING WITH
LOUIS ARMSTRONG
'68

The Hallway

Often overlooked as a space to simply pass through, time spent in the humble hallway is usually transient and fleeting. Yet it is the introduction to the rest of our home, setting the tone for what lies beyond its boundaries and offering a first unfiltered glimpse into our inner world.

Elevating the status of the hallway or entrance ensures we give this space the same weight and importance as the main rooms in our homes; it is, after all, the space that sees you off in the morning and greets you when you return. The entrance hall also provides a perfect opportunity to give new visitors a welcoming first impression; it whets their appetite and incites an inquisitiveness about the rest of your home.

It is easy to allow the unassuming hallway to fall short in our appraisal of spaces, which conventionally offer us an opportunity to hone our design skills and highlight our interior decoration. Prone to clutter, hallways all too quickly become an obvious dumping ground for shoes, bags, keys and piles of unopened mail. However, there are many ways in which to circumvent this hallway conundrum and save the space from becoming a drab, uninviting place relegated to cupboard status. See it instead as a moment for experimentation. A statement piece of artwork, a striking item of functional furniture or an unusual wall colour can transform the hallway into a vibrant and interesting space which draws people in to your home and creates the feeling that it is a room in its own right rather than simply a corridor to pass through.

FIRST IMPRESSIONS A contemporary ambience creates an interesting introduction to this London Edwardian terrace (opposite), where wall panelling painted in Farrow & Ball's 'De Nimes' adds impact, and art prints from PSTR Studio and Etsy draw the eye up the stairs. Antique furniture and an original oil painting greet those entering the hallway of my 1930s home (right).

A Characterful Prelude to Your Home

Whether you opt for a rich and resplendent space saturated in colour or a serene and composed ambience, the hallway is the preamble to the rest of your home, so all corners of this multifaceted space should be considered when designing the decor. By determining the kind of feeling you want to create when you – and any guests – first enter, you can begin to formulate a design scheme that embodies the essence of your home. Consider walls, lighting, flooring and furniture as individual elements that can bring character to the space as a collective, along with the decorative items you add as finishing touches. Also take into account any views into other rooms; there should be a a feeling of continuity and flow from the hallway into the rest of the house, achieved through both the colours and materials used and the style of decor.

Entrances come in all manner of shapes and sizes, so it is important to work with the space you have, and within the style of your home, and not overload it with superfluous furniture and decor or, conversely, leave it too spartan with little opportunity for storage and functionality. Here are some top tips for creating a hallway that is full of both personality and practicality.

Five Ways to Elevate your Hallway Decor

1 *Walls* – add character by introducing a warm colour, elegant wall panelling or a patterned wallpaper.

2 *Lighting* – consider multiple light sources, such as wall lights for a gentler glow, an overhead pendant light for illumination, and a table lamp for creating a welcoming ambience.

3 *Art* – add a statement piece that takes up one wall or perhaps arrange a gallery of artwork, photographs or illustrations.

4 *Furniture and storage* – if space permits, include a hallway table or sideboard that is aesthetically pleasing but also provides space for keys, a table lamp and some decorative objects. A bench with hidden storage or space for baskets underneath can provide a useful spot for storing everyday items.

5 *Flooring* – this should be hard-working but in keeping with the rest of the house; consider traditional flagstones or tiles, or durable wood with a patterned or jute rug for added colour and texture.

A WARM WELCOME Soft green walls painted in 'Ball Green' by Farrow & Ball welcome guests into the entrance hall of Glebe House in Devon (see page 120 to find out more), where a large, over-mantel mirror creates a focal point. Colourful ceramics and a quirky, contemporary, eight-shade chandelier add interest.

HALLWAY DESIGN Vintage Penguin books add interest in the home of Christen Pears (above), while warm tones and patterned wallpaper create a welcoming entrance in Anita Russell's home (opposite bottom left). Wall panelling painted in 'Mochi' by Little Greene is paired with 'First Signs' wallpaper by Studio Lecocq (opposite bottom right), and 'Lilou' wallpaper by Warner House is teamed with Lick's 'Beige 02' paint (opposite top left and right).

TOP DOGS
HOUSE BOOK
OLD HOUSE HANDBOOK
FLORA BRITANNICA
RICHARD MABEY
ANSELM KIEFER
OTTOLENGHI SIMPLE
TOM KERRIDGE'S FRESH START
Mary Berry
CAKE DAYS
THE COMPLETE AGA COOKBOOK
ULTIMATE TOYS FOR MEN
BOMB DAMAGE MAPS 1939–1945
BRANSON

PART THREE
Homes to Inspire

A Layered Aesthetic

A period spent looking after some of the world's most remarkable and exclusive homes inspired Holly Hardy's distinctive and eclectic approach to interiors. The 34-year-old, who shares a detached Edwardian property with husband Lewis and daughter Florence, has adorned her home with an array of globally sourced artwork and fabrics, creating a beguiling aesthetic. Set against a backdrop of vibrant wall colours, the pieces form an extensive and compelling collection, amassed by Holly over the last decade.

Holly's already burgeoning interest in one-of-a-kind art and homeware in her early twenties was fuelled by spending time managing the homes of celebrities and billionaires in London. 'It was such a fun job and many of the clients had a very distinctive style,' she recalls. 'Occasionally, we'd have a truly unique property in the portfolio, and it was always these that sparked my interest. I started noticing what made them special and how I could emulate that; there was a feeling of real individuality, a sense that nothing had been bought in the same place, era or even within the same budget. So, although I wasn't being educated by anyone as such, I was picking up tips and techniques on mixing and matching things to make a home feel fun and bespoke.'

Hunting out affordable art has become a pastime for Holly, who initially began looking for pieces in a bid to add colour and character to her somewhat bland first home. 'I started collecting artwork when I bought my first flat and everything felt so bare and cold without texture on the walls,' she says. 'I quickly realized that a piece of art, whether an oil painting or framed watercolour, could instantly add character, warmth and serenity to a home. I thought it incredible that you could spend anywhere from £10 to £1,000, and people often couldn't tell the difference, so I was able to fill the walls with artwork on my receptionist's budget each month; my home felt so inviting for very little money.'

Holly, who loves mid-century Swedish art and is rather fond of the odd nude painting, now sources many of her pieces at auction, but some of her favourites were lucky (and affordable) works from flea markets. 'My taste has changed as I've got older, but the artwork I still adore and cherish came from my early days of scouring antiques fairs and flea markets,' she points out. 'The large tree painting above my sofa in the living room was just £60 from eBay. My collection is now mainly Swedish; they are such emotive, eye-catching pieces and make our home feel alive. I love that they are all old, tell their own story, and I am just a small chapter in their lives. I would happily have many nudes on the walls too, but my husband isn't so keen!'

It was by chance that Holly discovered their period property, in a quaint East Sussex village in the UK, and was captivated by its idyllic location and charming features. 'Despite the dated decor and some necessary repairs, the house exuded a warmth and charm that drew us in,' says Holly. 'The spacious layout, natural light and original features, such as the floorboards, fireplaces and Edwardian windows, made it stand out. The position of the house felt pretty special too; we have a lovely pub nearby, privacy all around us, and a little stream in our woodland; it's very charming.' The elegant period features of the property offered Holly an inviting canvas on which to indulge her love of textures and layered decor. In every room, there are curious corners filled with artisan crafts and fabrics,

GLOBALLY INSPIRED A vintage Uzbekistan suzani stretched over a large canvas creates a striking wall hanging in Holly Hardy's drawing room, painted in Farrow & Ball's 'Lulworth Blue', where a striped sofa bought on eBay is furnished with an Indian kantha quilt and vibrant cushions. A 1970s Italian lamp base, sourced at a Swedish auction, is paired with a handmade Indian silk lampshade.

mementoes of Holly's time abroad. Hand-embroidered suzanis, used as throws and striking wall hangings, are interwoven with block-printed lampshades and curtains and vintage ceramics. 'I want my home to represent us and our story, but also to be playful and uplifting, with a mixture of patterns, colours and textures.'

Coming from a family of creatives – her sister is a decorative artist and her mother a crafting whiz – it is unsurprising that Holly has turned her passion for vintage fabrics and homeware into a business, Sourced by Holly. Working from a garden studio, Holly sources and sells one-of-a-kind fabrics, lampshades and cushions from around the world. She admits it is challenging to balance this venture with being a parent and renovating the rest of their home, but it satisfies her need to be innovative and immersed in all things interiors. 'Although I am useless at crafting, deep down I'm a real creative,' she says. 'I was discovering so many beautiful designs and products when kitting out our own home and began to form relationships with the artisans I was talking to around the world, so that's how the business started. I love the buying side of things; choosing new stock is what keeps it exciting. I am always on the hunt for a new product line, while developing ideas and working with incredible craftspeople around the globe to create something completely individual; it's a dream come true.'

Colour has played a noteworthy role in Holly's mission to create a characterful home interior. Farrow & Ball's 'Fruit Fool' provides a punchy backdrop to floor-to-ceiling bookshelves in the snug (see pages 84–5 and 92), a space that Holly describes as 'uplifting and joyous'. She adds: 'Our bold and bright snug is a wonderful space, with its large windows, clashing fabrics and textured accessories. At night, the warm pink makes it feel so cosy, like you're being hugged from all around.' Another favoured space is the light-filled drawing room (see pages 87 and 90–1); painted in Farrow & Ball's 'Lulworth Blue', a fresh mid-blue, which Holly has harmonized with the more energetic tones and textures of a large suzani hanging on the wall. The scheme is completed by a plethora of eclectic cushions, some of which were destined as stock for Sourced by Holly but have instead found a home on her sofas.

Holly will quite often use a painting as a starting point around which to design a scheme, taking its colours and tones and building the decor around these. 'The colours in the oil painting in our bedroom are divine; they are quite subtle individually but together they have an intense colouring,' she says. 'I drew inspiration for the rest of the room from some of these softer colours.'

Although using colour comes easily to Holly, becoming confident in mixing patterns has presented more of a learning curve. 'I once found fabrics intimidating,' she says. 'But my sister used to work for Colefax and Fowler, a brand renowned for their fabrics and wallpapers, so after some tips I was on a roll with mixing and matching patterns, scales and colours.' If a fabric is beyond her budget, Holly will use a less expensive, plainer design and add a decorative braid as a trim. 'This helps break up the simplicity of the linen and gives it more interest,' she explains. 'I have used the same trick in the entrance hall, as I wanted something quite neutral to go with the ever-changing tablecloths I use on the table for photographing stock, but I didn't want it to feel dull. Blue trim down the edge softens the look and gives it a bit of personality and style.'

Holly's home is infused with originality, but also feels comfortable and even a little playful. She approaches her roles – business owner, mother, renovator and art collector – with boundless enthusiasm as creating joyful interiors is just that: so very gratifying and joyous.

ECLECTIC BLEND A colourful portrait sourced in Sweden instantly captures the eye in the entrance hall to Holly's home (opposite) and is complemented by Farrow & Ball's 'Harissa', painted on the mantelpiece below. In the drawing room (overleaf), vintage fabrics and patterned cushions are juxtaposed against Farrow & Ball's 'Lulworth Blue'.

in my Life

COLLECTED CURIOS A vintage Swedish wall sconce creates an intriguing mix with more contemporary accessories, including a fabric lampshade by Alice Palmer & Co and patterned cushions, set against a background of Farrow & Ball's 'Fruit Fool' in the snug (above). An idiosyncratic mix of old and new decor (opposite) reflects Holly's keen eye for creating interesting interiors and sourcing original art, antique ceramics and artisan fabrics.

CONSIDERED DESIGN Bookshelves crafted into a fireside nook sit above a slipper chair from OKA in the entrance hall (opposite). The bookshelves are painted in Farrow & Ball's 'String', also used on the fitted cupboards. An antique writing bureau graces the drawing room (above), while a table from eBay and antique ladder-back dining chairs bring warmth to the dining room (overleaf). Here, an antique oil painting sits above a vintage Hungarian sideboard.

COHESIVE COLOUR An intuitive use of colour ensures there is continuity throughout the different spaces of Holly's home. Accents of mustard yellow and deep green, shown in the dining room (above) and in the kitchen area (opposite), punctuate the spaces with interest, while Farrow & Ball's 'Stone Blue' on a floor-to-ceiling glazed wardrobe (closet) creates a colourful and arresting corner in the primary bedroom of the cottage (overleaf).

CLASSIC DESIGN The primary bedroom (above) exudes a calm serenity, with walls painted in Farrow & Ball's 'Pointing'. A large oil painting of a French town, which Holly found at a flea market, sits above an antique chest of drawers. On the opposite page, Morris & Co wallpaper in 'Willow Bough' adds character to a washroom and is accented by Farrow & Ball's 'Inchyra Blue', which is used to striking effect on a door and the surrounding woodwork.

Slow Living, Mindful Comfort

Longing to find an antithesis to the turbulent times of her past, lawyer Kasturi Wren felt compelled to create mindful spaces within her home, filled with the quiet comfort of art, books and music. Having left behind a different existence and embarked on a new life of sequestered self-reliance, the 44-year-old needed her home to offer both solace and sustenance. 'This home was where I decided to start a new life,' says Kas of her 1910 white weatherboard cottage. 'I had just left a long marriage, along with the religion and community I grew up in, and then came out as a gay woman, so finding a new design for my own life required me to live in a space that gave me comfort and purpose. Over the years, I have dabbled in various interior design styles and decor, but this time I wanted a place that resonated with what made me happy; I wanted a place full of light, warmth, character and peace. I wanted a nest that resonated with a life of quiet and slow living.'

There is an ease with which Kas has designed her home; spaces feel considered, yet comfortable, familiar almost. It comes as no surprise that the three-bedroom cottage, in rural New South Wales, Australia, is often used as a retreat, with Kas opening her doors to travelling artists and the occasional young person seeking comfort and warmth. But her quintessential Australian country home, with its tin roof and verandah, was not always quite so comfortable. When Kas, who lives with her two dogs Willow and Alf, purchased the property, the house was gloomy and in need of a lot of work, despite being well loved by its former owners. But something about the 'bones' of the cottage drew Kas in. 'When I first saw the house, it was like many country homes, dark and uninsulated, but I felt the layers of love and a lifetime of stories etched into the walls,' recalls Kas. 'I could see a great deal of work would be needed to make the place warm and light, but I also saw all of its possibilities too.'

The transformation of Kas's home, which is nestled in the foothills of Australia's imposing Liverpool mountain range and surrounded by a large rose garden, took her just less than a year to complete. With the help of a local builder, nicknamed 'Handbag', Kas was able to reimagine many of the spaces within the property, which included flooding the house with natural light through the installation of two large new windows in the kitchen. For Kas, a former partner at Slater & Gordon, one of the largest consumer law firms in Australia, but who now enjoys the slower pace of running her own local legal practice, this room would become one of the most invigorating spaces in her home. 'The kitchen is where my day begins and where I find my centre,' she says. 'The morning light gives me a feeling that anything is possible; it is a restorative space.'

Evoking a relaxed Provençal style with its antique copper pans, hanging baskets and old wooden island, the kitchen's rustic tranquillity is in consummate harmony with its bucolic surroundings. An old black range cooker, once the only source of heat for the house and nestled in an original brick chimney breast, further enhances the classic country charm. A stunning eight-panelled window, sourced by Kas, dominates one side of the kitchen, framing the adjacent dining room and giving the two disparate spaces a connection. But it is the sizeable farmhouse sink, with its olive-green fabric skirt and traditional brass taps, that has become the heart and soul of Kas's kitchen. Not an easy

OPEN SPACES In a dining room corner, dog Willow perches on a cane chair from vintage traders Verandah Collective. An antique desk (see also page 112, top right) with a marble top, from Facebook Marketplace, sits in front of an eight-pane window, which frames a view through to the kitchen where a collection of hanging baskets adds texture and interest.

piece to come by, it was, like the sourcing of many treasured pieces, an exercise in determination and patience. 'It is almost impossible to find old sinks in Australia,' says Kas. 'I searched high and low for a business that sold old farmhouse sinks, before I found a place in Sydney that sourced and refurbished the most beautiful of sinks. I'm not sure how I managed to move it 400km (248 miles) but I did, and "Handbag", with a grinder in one hand and a cigarette in the other, made a beautiful frame for it. The sink is originally from Louisville, in Kentucky, and is such a statement piece for the kitchen; it has become the heart and soul of it.' Kas, whose family moved from Sri Lanka to Australia in 1987 to escape the civil war, painted the kitchen's wooden floors in a muted chequerboard design, a subtle nod to her love of understated pattern and calm colours. The space feels both well-used and useful, while character oozes from every corner.

A tempered colour palette of muted ochre, olive and monochrome tones plays out across walls, floors and furniture to create a unified feel – a well-considered scheme that seems to reflect the property's agricultural surroundings. Kas created the olive-green paint colour 'Coolah' in collaboration with Australian paint brand Murobond and uses it to full effect in her bedroom, where the colour carries down from the ceiling to the shiplap walls, softening conventional lines of distinction and creating a cocooning effect. Decor in this space is unfussy, giving key pieces room to breathe; a glazed cabinet, sourced on Facebook Marketplace and displaying favourite books and ceramics, is joined only by a wooden bed and velvet button-back armchair, which Kas bought at one of her favourite auction houses, Raffan Kelaher & Thomas, in Sydney.

Kas's uncomplicated approach to decor continues in the bathroom, where a black claw-foot bathtub sits on a wooden floor in a chequerboard design. Monochrome tones are softened by a long linen shower curtain hung from a ceiling-high rail. It is this interplay between rustic and minimal, and soft and textured, which creates both consistency and curiosity all through Kas's home. Artwork appears throughout the property, with favoured pieces including Hammershøi-inspired works by Australian artist Peter Boggs and *The Dapper* by New South Wales-based artist George Raftopoulos.

A masterclass in conscientious decorating, Kas's home feels curated, yet meaningful; each room has a clear purpose, while still exuding a feeling of quietude. 'I love how this home has spaces that feed a particular state of mind,' says Kas. 'The library, the garden room, the room to lay in the bath and listen to records, and also the room where food is created and people fed. In designing the interiors, I turned to my own artistic and creative instincts to make spaces that reflect where I am in life and what I think makes a quality life.'

Kas's love of creative endeavours, particularly words, is reflected in her extensive collection of books, which fill many corners of her home. Floor-to-ceiling bookshelves frame the open fireplace and establish a focal point in the living room, while whitewashed walls contrast with darker toned artwork and wooden furniture, creating a cosy space. 'Books have been the one constant in my life of transition,' says Kas. 'I'm content when there's a roast in the oven, the open fireplace crackling away, and my dogs curled up with me as I read a passage of poetry.' These are simple days filled with simple pleasures, and from which Kas derives great joy. 'This is a home in which to cook food, sit on the verandah and watch the garden and the heavens do what they do best out here: put on a show of endless skies,' says Kas. 'My home reminds me of my greatest promise to myself: to find peace, hold it, and live within it every day.'

RUSTIC CHARM A large, restored enamel sink adds vintage charm to Kasturi's kitchen, while a rustic wooden table grounds the space and provides a work surface for food preparation. The painted wooden floor features a chequerboard design in olive green. An eight-panelled window, sourced by Kasturi, frames the adjacent dining room and allows light to flow between both spaces.

LIGHT MEETS DARK A Danish antique table sourced at a Sydney auction house creates a compelling contrast against whitewashed walls in the dining room (above), while muted ochres and a collection of blue and white crockery displayed in a secondhand plate rack inject colour into the adjoining kitchen (opposite). An original brick chimney breast in the characterful kitchen is home to an old black range (previous pages).

TEXTURE & COMFORT Layers of wooden furniture and textured fabrics create a cosy retreat on a verandah (above), including a sofa from Sydney-based MCM House and a colonial armchair from antiques store Water Tiger, also in Sydney. An easel features artwork by Australian artist Kim Harding. An elegant side table, sourced at auction, adds interest to Kasturi's kitchen (opposite top left), while flowers lift the dining room (opposite bottom left and right).

SLOW LIVING Floor-to-ceiling bookshelves frame an open fireplace and establish a strong focal point in the living room (opposite), while whitewashed walls create contrast with woodwork painted in Murobond's 'Oyster'. The living room is also home to a display of artwork, including *The Dapper* by New South Wales-based artist George Raftopoulos, pieces by Australian landscape artist Peter Boggs and also an antique bird print (above).

SAMUEL TAYLOR
COLERIDGE
AN ANTHOLOGY

MONOCHROME TONES A black glazed cabinet sourced on Facebook Marketplace (opposite top right and above) displays favourite books and curios in the primary bedroom, where a velvet, button-back armchair from Sydney auction house Raffan Kelaher & Thomas adds texture. A pair of shoes from India, given to Kasturi as a gift, adds interest to shelving (opposite bottom left), while a dark-toned artwork contrasts with white walls in another bedroom (opposite bottom right).

MUTED COLOUR SCHEME An olive-green ceiling, painted in 'Coolah', a colour created by Kasturi in collaboration with Australian paint brand Murobond, continues a little way down the shiplap walls in the bedroom (above). Traditional claw-foot bathtubs are combined with industrial-style lighting and accessories in the bathrooms of the property (opposite), while an oversized chequerboard design on the floor of one of the bathrooms creates further impact.

Joyfully Eclectic

There's something undeniably intoxicating about the spaces within Glebe House, a glorious Georgian property set atop a hill in the middle of breathtaking English countryside. A sort of Bohemian eclecticism fills the rooms of the spacious five-bedroom former vicarage; a place where you might imagine artists, creatives and the well-travelled to convene and mull over their days.

Although not strictly an artist's residence in practice, it is, indeed, owned by one – Olive, a 37-year-old painter, along with her husband Hugo and their two young boys, Rufus and Robin. Stepping foot inside the 1700s property through the 'garden room', with its enormous grapevine extending happily into the roof space, is rather like entering an enchanted cottage from a childhood book. Curiosity then awaits at every twist and turn of this colourful home; the eye is drawn enticingly from one captivating space to another, looking at walls filled with original artwork as well as vintage ceramic vases and trinkets which are dotted around windowsills, shelves and cosy nooks. Every corner of this charming home implores you to linger a little longer, but, although there is a *laissez-faire* feeling to its relaxed and easy aesthetic, it began, like any finished space, of course, as just a vision.

Once city dwellers embodying the fast-paced existence of London life, Olive and Hugo gave up their day jobs in the capital – working in creative advertising and insurance, respectively – to return to Glebe House, Hugo's childhood home, with a view to transforming it into an individual place offering accommodation, home-grown food and creative experiences. These were ambitious plans for the property, situated as it is in the undulating hills of the idyllic Coly Valley, in East Devon, in the UK, and previously run as a B&B by 38-year-old chef Hugo's parents, but it was a vision into which the couple have ploughed four years of creative spirit and determination. 'Glebe is somewhere we would come and feel like there's just nowhere else quite like this,' says Olive. 'We had lived in London for 10 years and loved it, but we're both from the countryside and felt the pull to come back. I enjoyed my job in the city, but I was painting a lot in the evenings and weekends and wanted to be more physically creative with my hands. Coming back to Glebe was a good opportunity for us to create something for ourselves; it felt like a natural move.' Having a clear vision of what they wanted Glebe House to look like helped the couple harness their pipe dream and turn it into something tangible. 'We wanted to create something unique at Glebe, not just a place for people to stay, but a creative hub with an emphasis on art and soulfulness, somewhere people would feel inspired,' says Olive.

It is at once clear that colour is a defining thread running throughout the property's interior; a refreshingly unrestrained palette pervades the spaces, from the punchy pink-heavy drawing room, to the striped green walls of the dining room, and a cornucopia of hand-drawn wallpapers and murals in between. Such a superfluity of colour could be overwhelming but, conversely, creates an unexpected, yet delightful energy as one moves through the

STRIPES & SHELVES Oversized hand-painted stripes painted in 'Puck' by Little Greene create an eclectic feel in the dining room of Olive and Hugo Guest, while artwork by Olive adds a colourful focal point above the original fireplace of the former vicarage. Alcove shelving hosts an eye-catching collection of books, ceramics and glassware.

Food for Free
SECRET VINEYARDS of FRANCE
CHEESE
BOOK
modes
fish
Perfect Houseplants
Flourish

disparate spaces. Each room embodies its own personality, independent and free of the conventional restraints of a more prescriptive or pared-back colour scheme; a conscious design choice Olive was keen to implement. 'We wanted Glebe to have distinct rooms with their own characters, for each room to be a celebration of colour and pattern,' she explains.

Summers spent in Italy after her parents moved there when she was in her twenties also had a significant influence on Olive's choice of colours for the property. 'My parents moved out to Italy when I was 21 and I spent a lot of time there, and then when Hugo and I were first together, we would holiday in Italy. Those warm pastel colours you find in the landscape, houses and pottery over there undoubtedly inspired our colour choices at home.' Variations of those earthy terracotta colours that Olive loves so much have found their way into many of Glebe's spaces, including the drawing room where Farrow & Ball's vibrant and inviting 'Fruit Fool' makes an unabashed statement and provides a striking backdrop to the couple's impressive collection of antique furniture, artwork and ceramics. 'This felt like a really brave terracotta colour to use, and quite a big decision at the time,' says Olive. 'There's always that moment, before you've got anything else on the walls or in the room, where you think to yourself "Is it too much?" But actually, it's brought the space to life and it feels so warm and cosy; you walk into that room and it feels like you're being given a big hug.' A large, patterned chair found at an antiques centre and a vintage bamboo screen sourced from an online secondhand site add texture and intrigue to the room, alongside ceramics and trinkets collected over the years. It is these small, yet meaningful items that add layer upon layer of interest to the rooms in Glebe House and make the interiors so deeply individual.

RADIANT & UPLIFTING The family kitchen, designed by Neptune and featuring traditional oak cabinetry, is drenched in warm terracotta tones with Farrow & Ball's 'Fake Tan' on tongue-and-groove panelling and a red island painted in Neptune's 'Burnham Red'. The island chairs are vintage Scandinavian Brutalist bar-stools sourced on Etsy.

It was something of a foregone conclusion that art would be the nucleus of Glebe's interiors. Growing up with an artist mother and grandmother, Olive was surrounded by easels, painted furniture and murals. Her formative years were spent at her grandparents' eclectic home in Wiltshire – the interiors of which were reminiscent of the Bloomsbury Group residence, Charleston Farmhouse in Sussex, England, where every surface was considered a canvas – established in Olive an intrinsic imaginative expression and tendency towards artistic freedom. 'I remember visiting Charleston Farmhouse and it immediately made me think of my grandparents' home as my grandmother was always painting chairs or other pieces of furniture,' says Olive. 'There was this philosophy that home was like an ever-evolving creative experience; new art would be made, another wardrobe or chair might be painted, and then something else would be repainted to fit in with it. You don't realize it as a child, but that exposure to art and colour soaks into your psyche and becomes part of your DNA.'

The notion that art can embody all your interiors, and not simply be limited to a print or canvas hung on the wall, can be seen in the swirling flowers, abstract shapes and impressionistic works adorning much of Glebe House's furniture, doors and walls. Spaces are filled with a zestfulness that feels almost heady in its blatant rejection of formality, and interiors feel soulful and authentic. 'Home, for me, is a living piece of art that is always evolving; surrounding ourselves with art and painted furniture or walls makes me feel joyful.'

Whimsy is woven throughout the property through the recurrent use of patterned and floral wallpaper in a variety of modern traditional prints, with several of the rooms and en-suite bathrooms dressed in collections by independent design houses. The aptly named 'Tulip Room', petite in size yet packing a punch in vibrancy, features London-based Dutch designer Ottoline de Vries's playful 'Little Wild Tulips' wallpaper in a red and green colourway. The lively print creates a cosy backdrop to a French antique bed with a striking, mustard-coloured, velvet headboard, while original artwork by Olive in similar colours ensures a consistent colour palette and adds the finishing touch to the design scheme. A second Ottoline print can be found in the downstairs washroom, which features the designer's 'Chintz Constance' wallpaper in a green and lilac colourway, with added texture and colour from a fabric sink skirt in an ochre linen fabric.

Yellow tones are used consistently throughout the property and efficaciously create drama in the largest room, where a freestanding Burlington bath takes centre stage. The traditional bathtub is complemented by 'Daisy' wallpaper from Morris & Co, along with a bold yellow bedspread and canopy bed frame. It is a brave move to use so many different wallpapers in a home, but these are design schemes executed with confidence and delivered with consistent colour palettes within each space, and therein lies the key to successfully mixing and matching colour and pattern. 'I've always loved wallpaper,' says Olive, who worked with long-time friend and designer Ali Childs of Studio Alexandra on many of the design schemes within Glebe House. 'It adds a different element to a room and can be used to inject fun into a space, through the layering of patterns and colours.'

Perhaps one of the most important spaces to Olive and Hugo is the family kitchen; a radiant space drenched in warm terracotta tones. Inspired by the earthy clay shades of the nearby Jurassic cliffs, the couple wanted an uplifting space where they could cook and spend time with sons Rufus, four, and Robin, two. 'Planning this kitchen was an amazing process; it is such an important space for us as a family. We needed to make sure it was multifunctional but also somewhere we would enjoy cooking and the kids could do their thing and be with us at the same time,' says Olive. 'We spend a lot of time at the local beaches, so we wanted to bring those orange shades you find at the cliffs here into the house.' The kitchen, designed by Neptune, blends traditional oak cabinetry with a striking red island and Farrow & Ball's 'Fake Tan' on tongue-and-groove panelling. The space feels traditional, yet completely individual to Olive and Hugo.

The couple have come a long way since they first began dreaming about what Glebe House could one day become. With their fast-paced London life now far behind them, this intriguing old building has become more than just a home to Olive and Hugo; it is a place to experiment with artistic endeavours, to inspire and be inspired by its bucolic surroundings, and also an opportunity to teach their children about the joy that can be derived from creative expression. 'We've fallen into a happy rhythm at Glebe; we feel so connected to the seasons here and have embraced that slower pace of life you find yourself living in the countryside,' says Olive. 'We wanted to create something joyful at Glebe, a place where creativity and art breathe life into its spaces, and although it's been a challenge at times, I feel like we've really achieved that.'

TONE & TEXTURE Terracotta flooring blends with the warm tones of the oak cabinetry, while a capacious fluted Belfast sink adds a traditional element to the design of the kitchen (opposite). In the drawing room (overleaf), Farrow & Ball's 'Fruit Fool' creates a joyful background for vibrant artwork and antique furniture, including a patterned chair found at an antiques centre.

THE IMPRESSIONISTS
EMILY POWELL
PETER AND LINDA MURRAY
The Art of the Renaissance

COLOUR CONFIDENT Tongue-and-groove panelling painted in Farrow & Ball's 'Babouche' is paired with Sanderson's 'Archive' wallpaper, while a striking flower design embellishes the door (above). A colourful stair runner from The Cloth Shop complements a staircase painted in Farrow & Ball's 'Card Room Green' (opposite). Views over the Devonshire countryside create a captivating panorama in the 'garden room', complete with potted plants and a climbing vine (previous pages).

MISCELLANY OF PATTERN Wallpaper by Morris & Co in 'Daisy' brings energy to the bedroom (above and opposite bottom left), while Ottoline de Vries's 'Little Wild Tulips' wallpaper adds vibrancy to a smaller bedroom (opposite top left). A wardrobe, hand-painted in a Bloomsbury style by Olive, adds interest to a landing (opposite top right) and a headboard in fabric by Sophie Meade-Fetherstonhaugh brings elegance to another bedroom (previous pages).

ELEVATED DESIGN A freestanding Burlington bath painted in 'Babouche' by Farrow & Ball injects a feeling of luxury to the largest bedroom in this colourful 1700s property, while the small wooden chair sitting to one side adds a touch of quirkiness to the decor (opposite). 'Artichoke', a soft green by Paint & Paper Library, is used on both the door architrave and other woodwork in a small en-suite bathroom (above) off the bedroom shown on page 135, top left.

Cottage Calm

Memories of colourful Scandinavian beach houses, captured from a childhood spent growing up on the Norwegian coastline, have undoubtedly had a prevailing influence over Anita Russell's interior style. Her modest 1950s bungalow, which sits atop a hill in the Cotswolds, in the UK, would be just as much at home in the 36-year-old's motherland as it is in the English countryside.

Wood-clad walls provide a textured framework for a considered cottage aesthetic, where vintage wallpapers meld with earthy paint colours to evoke a subtle sense of nostalgia and whimsy. 'My style is heavily inspired by my Scandinavian upbringing,' explains Anita, an interiors photographer and stylist. 'I grew up on the coast in Norway in old wooden houses and have always wanted to create a similar style in the UK. I have such clear memories of a little house that belonged to my mum; each room was painted in a different colour and there was a rustic kitchen painted in cornflower blue, with a mishmash of cupboards that had been gathered over years and put together to create a kitchen. Maybe that's why I like mixing old and new; I don't tend to jump on big trends but rather choose items that make me happy or have a story behind them.'

Anita, who lives with her husband and two daughters, spent six years transforming their bungalow into a carefully curated family home, tackling many of the renovations herself. The desire to create a comfortable and authentic dwelling goes far beyond a yearning for aesthetically pleasing interiors, however; 'home' is a word that conjures up deep feelings of security and belonging for Anita, but for a long time it was synonymous with something quite different. As a child, family life was difficult and often filled with chaos and uncertainty. Anita and her mother moved many times, never settling in one property for very long; as a result, forming a connection with her surroundings is something Anita has struggled with in the past. Despite many happy memories of her Scandinavian childhood by the sea, home life did not get any easier as she grew older, and Anita ended up in foster care from the age of 11 until she was 18. 'Nothing felt like home for long periods of time when I was a child,' explains Anita. 'Family life was difficult, and me and my mum had to move around quite a lot. I never felt like I belonged anywhere, and then I moved into foster care at 11 and that feeling followed me until I was a young adult. I was lucky to move into some really lovely Scandinavian homes, but that joy was often short-lived, and we would move on.'

A chance encounter on a Spanish beach, when she was 23, changed the course of Anita's life for ever. 'It wasn't until I met my husband on a beach in Spain that I felt like, yes, this is how it is to feel at peace and to have a real feeling of belonging. I moved to the UK the following year and, although we also moved around a lot here, we eventually found a place that felt like home in the Cotswolds.' Surrounded by hills and undulating valleys, small quintessentially English villages, towns

COSY COMFORT A window seat crafted by Anita from offcuts of wood creates a cosy seating area in the living room, while a cushion from Barker and Stonehouse introduces a relaxed pattern to the space. A wooden bowl found in a home clearance store for only £15, and displayed on a coffee table, adds warmth and texture, while floral art prints adorn the walls.

and hamlets, Anita finally felt a sense of belonging, and for the first time, a compulsion for permanence led to 'home' becoming a place of safety and security. 'When I had my first child 12 years ago, everything changed. I needed to provide stability and give my children a home that felt safe and permanent; a sanctuary to escape to, if needed, or a place to curl up and just "be" without the pressure of outside noise and distractions. To finally have a safe space that is ours is all I've ever wished for.'

That unshakeable need to create a sanctuary of her own is perhaps why Anita has thrown herself unreservedly into transforming the once 'bland and soulless' bungalow. One space that brings her unsurpassable joy is the kitchen; with its handmade, ceiling-height open shelves created in their entirety by Anita and her power tools, earthy paint tones and vintage kitchenware, it is a warm, welcoming hub for family and friends. A simple dining table sits off to one side; more than just a place to eat at mealtimes, it signifies happier times from Anita's childhood. 'I grew up sitting around the kitchen table listening to my family talk about their days over a cup of coffee,' she reminisces. 'In Norway, a kitchen table by the window is a must; family and friends would gather around the table, while the coffee brews, and chat about the world outside, which would normally be a man on a tractor or a fishing boat.'

Every corner of the kitchen has been considered and curated to maximize practicality, but also visual interest and a sense of homeliness. Terracotta pots filled with cooking utensils and aged wooden chopping boards sit atop a rustic wood countertop, while a fabric kitchen skirt adds a touch of whimsy, cleverly hiding unsightly appliances. Tongue-and-groove panelling painted in 'Mochi' by Little Greene adds depth and texture to the walls, enveloping its occupants in warm, autumnal tones. 'It's the perfect muted, warm colour, almost like a hug,' says Anita, who cites nature as the biggest inspiration behind her colour palette. 'Nature is very inspiring for me when it comes to choosing paint colours; I find muted tones easier to pair together. I love being outside and often go for long walks in the countryside. If you look at the colours that surround you, you'll notice how well they all work together; nature does it best.'

In the hallway, delicate, small-scale wallpaper from Warner House in a honey colourway is teamed with wood panelling in a soft, earthy tone courtesy of Lick's 'Beige 02', providing a warm welcome into the two-bedroom property. The use of wallpaper is continued throughout Anita's home; vintage-inspired designs soften the spaces, while creating continuity through the disparate rooms. In a nod to nostalgia, Anita credits a childhood friend's colourful beach house on a small Norwegian island as the inspiration behind her wallpaper choices. 'I remember dearly my friend's holiday cabin on a gathering of islands right in the Atlantic Ocean; it was a little cottage painted red with white frames around the windows and had a rugged garden with heather shrubs and ferns growing wild,' she recalls. 'Every room had a different wallpaper and the top bedrooms under the eaves all had their own colour scheme. One had baby-blue woodwork and blue wallpaper to match, along with a beautiful antique sled

LAYERS OF INTEREST A gallery of artwork, including prints by American artist Carleigh Courey, makes for an eye-catching focal point against a backdrop of 'Beige 02' from Lick on the walls of Anita's living room. The wicker chair, bought secondhand from charity The Home Remedy, has been paired with a cushion from Amazon, while a rug from Dunelm adds to the a layered feel.

bed with crocheted bedspreads and a chest of drawers with hand-painted flowers on it. The other room was light yellow with a delicate floral wallpaper that went all the way up the sloped ceilings and a small window on one side of the room, overlooking the sea. It was my idea of heaven to visit this place every summer and other holidays.'

A rustic moodiness fills the primary bedroom, with Benjamin Moore's 'Mountain Moss' mirroring the colours of the bungalow's rural location on the wooden-clad walls. A vintage chest of drawers, thrifted from a local antiques store, adds understated charm and character to the space, while a softly pleated wall lamp in pale ivory, which belonged to Anita's grandmother, brings a welcome contrast to the dark walls.

Anita's love of vintage may have come from a need to furnish the family's home on a budget, but it is also fuelled by a passion for one-off pieces which have their own sense of identity. 'I love the signs of wear and tear, like they are telling a story from a different lifetime,' she says. 'I think those pieces are so beautiful and a real talking point for people when they visit. I don't think new furniture has that same soul. There is a thrill searching for individual pieces instead of just ordering something new online; sometimes it can take months to find what you're looking for, but the wait is worth it when you find that special piece.'

The bungalow may be small in scale, but no corner has been left untouched. Anita delights in the beauty of the ordinary, balancing the need for functionality with a desire for items that are aesthetically pleasing. 'I feel happy if I am surrounded by beautiful things,' says Anita. 'Adding things to my home is my favourite pastime and over the six years we've been here, every single space has been considered. Sometimes, the things I bring to our home might not be new and fancy, but if it's functional as well as pretty, I'm happy with that. Because our home is very small, we don't have a lot of storage space, so most of our things are out on display, and that's why I always choose more beautiful things – for example, a wooden dustpan and brush over a plastic one. I find it's always the small details that count the most.'

Anita's vision for how she wanted her home to look and feel is less reverie and more manifestation; a combination of sheer hard work and imagination amounting to a transformation even the most seasoned of renovators would be proud of. 'We saw potential in this old bungalow and knew we could make it a lovely home over time,' says Anita. 'I liked that despite the bungalow not being a period property, it still had some lovely original floorboards, and everything else can always be added with a bit of imagination and determination. It has been such a joy to see a once bland and cold home being transformed into a cosy, cottage-like house with lots of character and soul. I've had to learn a lot of new skills, from wallpapering and tiling to using a drill, but I've enjoyed it. I want people to be surprised when they walk in the front door, because they might not expect our home to look this way when they see that it's just a little 1950s bungalow from the outside.'

KITCHEN DETAILS Tongue-and-groove panelling painted in 'Mochi' by Little Greene creates depth and interest in Anita's kitchen, while handmade, ceiling-height shelves provide an opportunity to display pots, pans and crockery. Wooden countertops add a rustic feel to the cottage-style kitchen, while weathered terracotta pots and plants add a hint of colour to the muted tones of this space.

SMØR

WARM TONES A display of wooden chopping boards adds visual interest, while a secondhand drop-leaf table provides a space-saving seating area in the kitchen (above). Ruffled, olive-green seat pads from Dunelm add softness both visually and physically, while utility skirts made by Anita herself (opposite) hide various kitchen appliances. In the cosy living room (overleaf), a Scandinavian-style scissor lampshade is mounted conveniently on the wall.

CREATE
CREATE
La France et les Français

WOODEN ELEMENTS A French-style walnut wardrobe by Laura Ashley (above), with rattan cane door and drawer fronts, brings understated elegance to the bedroom and creates consistency with other wooden elements, such as chests of drawers and a vanity unit, used in Anita's home (opposite). In the same room, wood-clad walls in Benjamin Moore's 'Mountain Moss' create an earthy palette alongside gingham bedding from Piglet in Bed (previous pages).

CAPTURE THE QUIET
FROM SEED TO BLOOM

Mid-Century Farmhouse

What started life as a serendipitous and somewhat humble collection of vintage paperbacks has become one of the most striking features of Christen Pears's captivating home. A 2,000-strong treasury of classic Penguin books fills floor-to-ceiling shelves in the living room of the 18th-century former farmhouse, their uniform of faded spines and sepia tones a prelude to the skilful mix of old and new that pervades the property's mid-century inspired interiors.

Books can be found in almost every space of Christen's home, situated a mere two miles from the breathtaking cliffs of the UK's untamed Cornish coastline, along with noteworthy curios and antiques collected from travels around the world with husband Chris, a former captain of tall ships. It is perhaps the enduring and stoic presence of both her impressive collection of books and vintage furniture which reveals Christen's compulsion for pieces that have a story to tell and offer a window into an alternate world. 'I've always loved reading; books are a part of your identity, particularly if they've been with you for many years, and they bring a sense of your personality to your home,' says Christen, a former journalist. 'I have a strong emotional attachment to my books and find it comforting and reassuring to have them around me.'

Low-key comfort percolates from the carefully curated items of decor that Christen has meticulously hand-picked for the spaces of her home, each piece bringing a truly individual offering to the eclectic, yet considered interior scheme. Hugely inspired by Scandinavian design, much of Christen's decor has been sourced on eBay or online vintage marketplaces, including Pamono and Vinterior. 'I love mid-century design, particularly Scandinavian design,' says Christen. 'My favourite designer is Børge Mogensen, a renowned Danish furniture designer; I've collected a lot of his pieces over the last few years, and I think his designs are the perfect embodiment of form and function. I particularly love the 2213 sofa in the living room, as it is such an iconic piece of furniture.' Another much-loved piece is a 1940s Ernest Race DA1 chair, which Christen had reupholstered in green fabric and makes for a stylish, yet comfortable companion to the wall of books in the living room. 'I buy predominately vintage because I love the patina and the quality, plus it also has less impact on the environment,' adds Christen.

A somewhat traditional exterior belies the intriguing spaces that lie within the property, where exposed stone is melded with sleek and contemporary wooden staircases, reminiscent of a snug Scandinavian ski chalet. An abundance of texture and wood tones creates a cosy ambience and shrewdly tempers the juxtaposition of more contemporary elements, which punctuate the spaces with a discerning sense of novelty. Walls have been kept neutral, with colour and pattern making a subtle statement in the soft furnishings and accessories, while rugs and blankets create a warm, layered aesthetic. 'Although I love Nordic interiors and they've inspired my decor, I've found that a predominately white scheme doesn't work for me; however, neutral tones paired with colourful accessories do,' explains Christen. 'I love texture because of the warmth and sense of depth it brings to a room, so I use a lot of rugs and blankets to add extra layers to the space.'

SLEEK DESIGN Handmade cabinets crafted from Dinesen Danish flooring planks and stained black contrast strikingly with Carrara marble countertops in Christen's kitchen. Open shelving displays Christen's kitchenware collection, including pieces from the Leach Pottery and Robert Welch and Japanese cooking utensils from Christen's travels overseas.

Nigel Slater
SEA & SHORE
SIMPLE
DIANA HENRY
HOW TO EAT A PEACH
DIANA HENRY
FOOD from PLENTY
DIANA HENRY
ROAST FIGS SUGAR SNOW
DIANA HENRY
FROM THE OVEN TO THE TABLE
DIANA HENRY
change of appetite
DIANA HENRY
NIGEL SLATER
NIGEL SLATER
Nigel Slater
the kitchen diaries
4th
Nigel Slater
The kitchen diaries II
4th
NIGEL SLATER'S REAL FOOD
Nigel Slater
NIGEL SLATER REAL COOKING
HOW TO EAT
NIGELLA LAWSON

Despite the now highly individual interior, it wasn't love at first sight when Christen first viewed the property over a decade ago. After living abroad for several years, both in Bermuda and Australia, the couple wanted to lay down more permanent roots in the UK. 'I had begun to miss England, so we began looking for somewhere with holiday accommodation, so we could enjoy a better work/life balance,' explains Christen. 'I had a shortlist of houses across the South West and this was the first one I saw. It wasn't exactly what I was looking for; I wanted somewhere with lots of period features, but I loved the location, the accommodation and the fact it had space for a Pilates studio and a walled garden.'

One of three farms once belonging to a larger estate, the property was sold after the First World War before a builder acquired it in the 1980s and converted the outbuildings into accommodation. Christen and husband Chris, who share their home with cats Robie, Vesper and Aida, bought the old farmhouse and smaller buildings in 2013 and began a full-scale renovation, which included replacing an old extension and turning the outbuildings into self-contained holiday lets. The bucolic plot, nestled down a quintessential winding Cornish lane and boasting an array of exotic plants native to England's southwestern tip, features a beautiful walled garden, along with a fitness studio and three idyllic holiday cottages, from where Christen often hosts various fitness retreats and reading parties.

Within the grounds is also a large barn, where Christen's enduring love of books and mid-century design continues to reign. The space has an almost otherworldly feel with a large library dominating one end and an open fire and seating area at the other. This features more of Børge Mogensen's designs, including the masterful and iconic Spanish Chair and the versatile J39 Chair. 'The barn has come a long way; it was falling down when we moved in and the surveyor actually recommended pulling it down,' recalls Christen. 'I originally planned it as a home office, but it became a library in the end. It feels like quite an indulgent space at times, especially in the colder months when you can light the fire and settle down for a few hours with a book.'

One of the most striking spaces in the property is the kitchen, with its handmade doors crafted from Dinesen Danish flooring planks, which Christen stained black, combined with beautiful Carrara marble countertops. Flooded with natural light and featuring

TRADITIONAL DESIGN Fresh green cabinetry in Little Greene's 'Jewel Beetle' creates a colourful aesthetic in the scullery, where a large butcher's block crafted from reclaimed wood provides a practical preparation area (opposite). The space is also home to a striking cream storage cupboard (right). Around 2,000 classic Penguin titles fill floor-to-ceiling bookshelves in the living room (overleaf), where a vintage Ernest Race DA1 chair provides an opportune reading spot.

a full-height wall of exposed stone, the kitchen, although a self-contained area, boasts a large opening onto the adjoining dining room, allowing for a seamless continuity of space between the two areas. 'One of the things I particularly admire about Scandinavian design is the way functionality and aesthetics go hand in hand; it was definitely something that I wished to achieve with the kitchen here,' says Christen. 'Because of the open-plan layout, I wanted the kitchen to relate to the dining room and also to the rest of the house.' Open shelving creates an opportunity for an eye-catching display of Christen's beloved pottery collection, many pieces of which come from world-renowned ceramicists the Leach Pottery, based in St Ives, just down the road from the couple's home. 'Having a scullery means that I can keep all of the really practical stuff hidden out of sight, so I chose open shelving for the kitchen,' explains Christen. 'It houses some of my collection of vintage Robert Welch pieces as well as practical pieces from the Leach Pottery and other bits and bobs like Japanese kitchen utensils and a casserole dish (Dutch oven) by influential Finnish designer Timo Sarpaneva.'

The scullery is a curious little space off the kitchen, where a hard-working butcher's block crafted from reclaimed wood is combined with fresh green cabinetry, painted in Little Greene's 'Jewel Beetle'. It has the feel of a diminutive Victorian cottage kitchen and embodies a softer, more whimsical atmosphere than the rest of the house, with its traditional Belfast sink, kitchen skirts and impressive collection of copper pots. Interestingly, despite its older feel, the space is part of the extension that Christen and Chris added to the property. 'Although it's new, the scullery has a more traditional feel than the rest of the house, but there is some continuity with the rest of the interiors,' explains Christen. 'The slate floor echoes the slate in the porch, the large cupboards are built with floorboards reclaimed from upstairs in the house, and the green paintwork picks up on the green accents elsewhere in the house.'

Christen has curated her home with such authoritative flair – an aptitude and mettle that speak of someone well versed in favoured design styles, able to apply their influences with aplomb to engender an individual and authentic interior scheme. But forging a definitive style has not always come naturally to Christen, to which she will attest. 'I remember when I decorated my first flat; I was in my early twenties and had no money and absolutely no idea what I was doing,' recalls Christen. 'I'd never decorated anything in my life and was slightly terrified, I suppose, of making a mistake, so I painted everything beige and bought off-the-shelf flatpack furniture.' It would be a move to the other side of the world where the couple became custodians of a beautiful Australian period property that cultivated a lifelong passion for interiors for Christen. 'We had a wonderful Federation house in East Fremantle, in Perth, and I started reading interiors magazines and did an interior design diploma online,' she explains. 'I was very into Art Deco at that time but there were also a few shops selling mid-century furniture nearby; my first purchase of this style of decor was a set of Danish teak candlesticks, and I've never looked back.'

Christen's journey with interiors has led her to uncover a prevailing passion for mid-century design that has formed the foundation of her own design schemes, applied in a measured, yet imaginative way to create a truly individual home. 'When it comes to interiors, I think you should follow your instincts and let your personality shine through. I've learned such a lot over the years, about designing an interior and my own tastes, and I'm not afraid to express them,' says Christen.

AUTHENTIC STYLE A trio of teak candlesticks, bought during Christen's time living in Australia, add height to a bespoke dining table, teamed with vintage Arne Jacobsen Grand Prix dining chairs (opposite). A mid-century modern sideboard by Clausen & Søn, also bought in Australia, creates a bold focal point against original stone walls (overleaf).

ALFRESCO
1992
GRACHTENHUIZEN
MASSERIA
ROOM 606
JOSEF FRANK
Remodelista
HOME MATTERS

KINFOLK

SCANDINAVIAN
FURNITURE
AT HEAL'S

THE ART OF DRESS
KURT JACKSON
HOKUSAI
ART DECO
HOPPER
RAVILIOUS
PENGUIN SPECIAL
PHIL BAINES PENGUIN BY DESIGN
BACKGAMMON
IL DOLCE FAR NIENTE
What Makes a Garden
JENNY ROSE-INNES

BEETHOVEN
MOZART
ELIZABETH I
THE STONES OF VENICE
THE GREEK MYTHS I
THE GREEK MYTHS II
HISTORY AND ROMANCE
HEROES AND SAINTS
The Moon's a Balloon
CIVILISATION
Nelson and Emma
WONDERS OF THE WORLD
ARTHUR
JAMES
FAREWELL THE TRUMPETS
Oxford
GHOSTLAND
BEST HOUSES
LEONARD COHEN
LANCASTER
KOBBÉ'S Complete OPERA Book
The Penguin Guide to Compact Discs
WAGER

BUTTER ASAKO YUZUKI

HIDDEN LIBRARY A converted barn with a cosy seating area (above and opposite) makes for an impressive home library painted in Farrow & Ball's 'Mole's Breath'. Vintage Hans J Wegner GE290 plank chairs are combined with a Moroccan wall hanging from Maroc Tribal (above). Børge Mogensen shelves, sourced from Pamono, house more of Christen's books (previous page). In the main house (overleaf), wood features feel sleek and modern against exposed stone walls.

MIXED ELEMENTS In the main bathroom (above), a bathtub from the Cast Iron Bath Company, painted in Farrow & Ball 'Railings', is complemented by Carrara marble tiles from Mandarin Stone and a concrete sink from Kast Concrete Basins, while a vintage Børge Mogensen chest of drawers from Pamono creates warmth in the primary bedroom (opposite top and below right). Metal bed frames also feature in other bedrooms (opposite below left).

The Bell Tower

Ascending the steep 200-year-old spiral staircase of The Bell Tower feels a little as if one has fallen into the opening pages of a fantastical tale. Original granite steps wind ever skywards until the doorway of Apartment One comes into view; as entrances go, this is about as intriguing as they get. Nestled within one of the most eclectic and creative hubs in Penzance, The Bell Tower is among the most iconic buildings in the UK's westernmost coastal town. Not to be outdone by the tower's fairytale façade, the interiors of the apartment fuse design-led decor with breathtaking vistas over the harbour below.

In stark contrast to the dark and enigmatic stairway, the apartment opens up into an airy, light-filled space where a pair of spectacular, six-foot-high, arched windows command attention and cosy window seats beckon one to sit awhile and absorb the all-encompassing panorama. A contemporary colour palette and sleek mid-century furniture create a curious juxtaposition with the tower's Georgian origins, yet the unfussy aesthetic of this historic hideaway invites a feeling of contemplative calm. It is an ambience that was central to owner Christen Pears's vision for this remarkable space. 'When we started renovating the apartment, I wanted to make sure we made the most of the amazing light and, of course, the view,' says the 49-year-old. 'I love the arched windows at the front, in particular. It's a great vantage point for watching what's going on in the harbour. Despite the height, it's such a welcoming space and always makes me feel relaxed.'

A renovation of fairly epic proportions took The Bell Tower, built in 1834, from dated and dire 1980s decor to a contemporary and chic living space that judiciously embraces original features, while weaving a subtle modernity through its contours. The striking building embodies a fascinating history, having started life as Cornwall's first National School before being turned into council offices in the 1960s and subsequently converted to apartments in the 1980s. It was finally given a makeover worthy of its distinctive architectural history in 2023, when Christen and husband Chris stripped the apartment bare and began uncovering the true value of its hidden attributes. 'The apartment hadn't been touched for around 40 years, so it was very dated,' recalls Christen. 'I wanted to preserve as much of the original features as possible but also create a canvas for my mid-century furniture. We had to strip everything out and start again. It was particularly satisfying to uncover some of the original features.'

A false floating ceiling was pulled down to reveal stunning original ceiling boards, the true height of which had been masked for several decades by unsightly polystyrene tiles. The original 190-year-old floorboards were also uncovered during the works; fortuitously hidden and consequently preserved by old carpet and lino, they were in excellent condition and have since become one of the apartment's most striking features. The entire floorplan was reworked to establish an open-plan living and kitchen area, maximizing the lofty feel of the apartment and flooding the space with natural light.

DESIGN-LED DECOR An iconic 1940s Poul Cadovius wall-mounted desk paired with an Arne Jacobsen Series 7 Swivel chair sits adjacent to the tower's impressive arched windows (opposite). In the apartment's kitchen (overleaf), a 19th-century French prep table is blended with contemporary IKEA units with simple oak cabinet doors by Custom Fronts.

Uncomplicated, yet beautiful in its simplicity, the kitchen occupies one end of the apartment, modest oak cabinetry blending harmoniously with the smooth lines of the mid-century decor that defines the design scheme. The unassuming IKEA units are a shrewd choice in sustaining an equilibrium between the architectural features of the property and the furnishings within it, with neither one competing for attention but rather maintaining an unpretentious and sympathetic balance. 'I was torn between a traditional Shaker kitchen and something with a more mid-century vibe,' says Christen. 'We were on quite a tight deadline, so in the end I opted for IKEA units with simple oak doors by Custom Fronts, who manufacture kitchen doors.' Open shelving crafted from an old school lab bench and adorned with simple pieces of pottery and kitchenalia piques the interest and adds a low-key sense of personality to the space.

A subtle quietude emanating from the pared-back and predominately modern design scheme is casually interrupted by unexpected period pieces which provoke intrigue and induce conversation. One such item is an imposing 19th-century French prep table which slices through the kitchen space and serves as a handy island; its aged patina provides a welcome contrast to the contemporary cabinetry. Its antiquity feels simultaneously discordant, yet wholly appropriate sandwiched within such modernity; the pairing is an illustration of how to strike an authentic balance between old and new decor, where neither element stifles the other.

Central to the apartment's distinctive decor are key mid-century pieces by renowned Danish furniture designers Børge Mogensen and Poul Cadovius; their individual and functional designs work well to maximize practicality and aesthetics across the open-plan floor space. A 1940s Cadovius wall-mounted desk, paired with an iconic Arne Jacobsen Series 7 Swivel chair, creates an eye-catching, yet space-saving workspace. In the living area, curves and colour come courtesy of Mogensen's classic Spoke-Back Sofa, a cosy piece with bright green upholstery and a gently curved frame designed to gracefully angle its occupants towards one another. Almost all of the vintage furnishings in the apartment have been sourced from online marketplaces, including Pamono, Vinterior and the Danish Homestore, some pieces requiring a little more patience than others in a bid to obtain them, but almost certainly worth the wait.

Beneath the quiet repose of the apartment lies the hustle and bustle of one of Penzance's most quirky and characterful streets, an area buzzing with boutiques, antiques stores and cosy eateries. Its eclecticism marries well with the idiosyncrasy of The Bell Tower, a felicitous blend where location, architectural detail and well-executed interior design meld together to create something rather special. The former school, now a sophisticated bolthole, which can be booked for short stays or holidays, combines historical relevance with an individual interior; it is, indeed, a truly unique little corner of Cornwall. 'I love everything about The Bell Tower,' says Christen. 'It feels like such a privilege to own part of this quirky and historic building.'

SHAPE & COLOUR A vintage Børge Mogensen blue day bed from Alto Stile is complemented by Little Greene's 'Etruria' painted on the frame of a window installed by Christen to allow daylight to flood into the bedroom beyond (opposite). Another splash of colour is provided by a Mogensen Spoke-Back sofa in the living area (overleaf).

YAHTZEE
SCRABBLE
MONOPOLY

CALM & SERENE Walls painted in Little Greene's 'Bone China Blue' create a soft ambience in the apartment's bedroom (above). They are accompanied by cupboards painted in 'Etruria', also from Little Greene, along with a simple bed frame from Heal's. Fresh green tiles from Mandarin Stone continue the contemporary feel in the adjoining bathroom (opposite), with wall lights from Corston Architectural Detail illuminating the sink area.

Colourful Converted Barn

Confronting a lack of direction in her life, at the age of 47, Charlotte Gaisford went back to college and became a student again. A brave move to embark on a new career maybe, but driven by an insatiable need to be creative, the mother-of-two reignited a lifelong love of artistic design and began a degree in textile design. Fast-forward more than a decade and Charlotte's home, a 150-year-old converted barn and cottages in the beautiful Northumberland countryside, is filled with her own striking fabrics and wallpapers, now coveted around the world.

From passion and determination was born an internationally successful business, which the 59-year-old manages, alongside a couple of staff, including a life-long friend, from outbuildings surrounding the barn. 'When I finished renovating the house, I was at a loose end and didn't know what I was going to do going forward,' says Charlotte. 'I always regretted not going to art school, so I decided to do a textile degree at the local college. I was old enough to be the other students' mother, but I loved it. I've been a creative person for as long as I can remember; I wanted to be an artist or a musician when I was younger, but being an artist was the dream really.' Charlotte has worked tirelessly to make her dream a reality, driven simply by her love of imaginative and creative endeavours. 'I very much enjoy what I do; it doesn't feel like a job to me,' she explains. 'Being creative is a joy. Seeing the finished article is important to me; I love to see the reaction on people's faces.'

Charlotte's eponymous collection of wallpaper and fabrics, inspired by anything from museum trips to everyday objects and which fuse both traditional and modern motifs in bold colours, have gained a loyal following in interiors circles and on social media. Adorning almost every surface in her home, Charlotte's lively designs, often named after influential people in her life, can be found on cushion covers, lampshades, wallpapers and curtains; the resulting aesthetic is a vibrant clash of patterns. 'I'm always amazed at the design journey my work takes me on, from creating the initial design to putting it on fabric and wallpaper, and then using those to decorate a room,' says Charlotte, whose love of pattern play is only equalled by her love of colour. 'I really can't do calm and neutral; I love bright colours because, for me, they help a room come alive.'

Meticulous to the end, Charlotte also does all her own decorating and wallpapering in the six-bedroom home. 'I am forever changing my interiors; there is always a project going on somewhere,' laughs Charlotte. 'I find it relaxing doing my own rooms; it's so satisfying doing a space from start to finish, and I will often have a good clear-out at the same time, so I can feel less burdened by life's rubbish, which can accumulate from time to time.'

Delightfully energetic, Charlotte's interior style elicits a feeling of curiosity not simply because of its bold take on maximalism meets classic English decor, but through its juxtaposition with the property's role as a working farm. Once owned by notable Northumberland family, the Riddells, and dating back to the 1880s, the estate on which Charlotte's home resides has been in husband Tom's family for generations. The couple spent eight months converting a large barn and two cottages into a single property, although it retains a 'quirky' layout with several corridors and hallways connecting the once disparate spaces. 'It was in a

CONTEMPORARY MEETS RUSTIC Bright cabinets contrast with original wooden beams in the kitchen of this converted barn (opposite), while a vibrant splashback – featuring 'Piccadilly Rouge', one of Charlotte's coveted wallpaper designs, protected with a clear acrylic screen – adds colour and pattern above a red Lacanche range oven.

BREAD

BREAD

sorry state before we did any building work,' recalls Charlotte. 'It took around three months of knocking out before we could start building again, although we tried to keep all the original openings. It really was very farm-like; the animals had just left when we began work.'

Despite being completely reimagined, the old farm buildings offer the occasional nod to their former life, mainly through family memorabilia displayed proudly throughout the property. Large portraits of ancestors in the drawing room, which is painted in Edward Bulmer's 'Invisible Green', help add context and a visual aide-memoire to some of the building's former occupants. 'I love seeing the faces of our family portraits and those of my ancestors; I often wonder what their lives were like in those days,' says Charlotte, mother to Harry, 25, and Richard, 23. 'I have to have old things in my home; pieces that tell a story. I'm lucky to have inherited some wonderful antiques. You can create such atmosphere in your home by combining pieces from different periods.' It is this injection of nostalgia, combined with Charlotte's love of colour and pattern play, which gives her home so much individuality and character.

As bold as she is brave with colour and pattern, Charlotte is firm on certain rules of thumb when designing a room scheme. 'When it comes to using pattern, you have to think about scale,' she advises. 'Start with a showstopper fabric for the curtains or headboard, if doing a bedroom, then look for smaller-scale patterns with a stripe or spot formation,' she explains. 'One of the biggest mistakes I think people make with pattern is thinking they should only use one

SIMPLE PALETTE The kitchen cabinets (opposite top left and right) are painted in 'Spanish Blue' by Craig & Rose. Panelling painted in 'Barns Green' by Albany is paired with Charlotte's wallpaper 'Dreaming Garden Green' in one of the four hallways (opposite below). In the drawing room (overleaf), Edward Bulmer's 'Invisible Green' on the walls is complemented by red accents from curtains in Charlotte's 'Rosie Open Red' fabric.

fabric for the whole room. They might add some lovely curtains but not consider the other soft furnishings, such as cushions or lampshades.' Colour is always a key part of Charlotte's design, but an unfussy palette is crucial to making the aesthetic work. 'I usually keep the colour palette simple; blue, green and red are my go-to colours,' she says. 'I often create a mood board, so I can see what all the different components of the room will look like; it's really important to consider how everything will work together in the one space.'

Charlotte's creative journey has been filled with dynamic encounters, TV appearances and intriguing business ventures. It was an 80-year-old nun at a convent in the Scottish Borders who first set the course for Charlotte's propulsion into the art world. 'I loved my art lessons with Sister Loretto,' Charlotte recalls. 'I remember her as a sweet little nun who wore sensible shoes. I got an 'A' in my A-Level Art exam, which was difficult to achieve in those days. I was so pleased as I wanted to make her proud.' Some years later, a second twist of fate saw Charlotte emerge from a 'disastrous' first marriage into a self-made businesswoman whose skills with a paintbrush opened doors to the television industry. 'After I left my husband, I had no money but a house that needed decorating,' she recalls. 'I couldn't afford wallpaper, so I started painting trees on my kitchen walls and the ceiling. I taught myself how to do paint effects and set up a shop offering paint services, as well as selling equipment and materials for paint effects.' Charlotte went on to travel the UK and Europe painting walls and furniture before landing an 18-part TV series for Sky TV, along with developing painting courses which were televised for BBC2's *The Art Show*.

Somewhere in between the difficult times and the highs of success, there has been one constant for Charlotte: her love of home and the need to create. 'I lost a home that was important to me when my marriage broke down,' says Charlotte. 'We had built a home together and I was devastated to leave very suddenly. But it made me realize I could create my own home anywhere.'

LEATHER

PATTERNED WALLPAPERS Warm tones flood a narrow hallway with Charlotte's 'India Red' wallpaper and woodwork painted in Farrow & Ball's 'Red Earth' (above), while 'Sharanshar' red wallpaper, also designed by Charlotte, envelops the entrance hall (opposite). A deep windowsill, in Farrow & Ball's 'Stone Blue', sets off a window overlooking lawns (opposite top left). A guest bedroom (overleaf), pairs Charlotte's 'London Birds' wallpaper with curtains in her 'Ionian Blue' fabric.

ECLECTIC COLLECTION Traditional meets modern in a twin bedroom (above), where Charlotte's 'Elizabeth Blue' wallpaper is paired with Farrow & Ball's 'Stone Blue'. Charlotte's wallpapers 'Sharanshar' and 'Picadilly Rouge' are also used (opposite top left and right), while the primary bedroom features her 'Pimlico Rouge' (bottom left). A portrait of Charlotte's husband's great-great-grandfather creates a powerful statement in a washroom (opposite bottom right).

INTERIORS
JACQUES GRANGE

Yesteryear Charm

It's 6am and a swathe of golden autumn sunlight filters through The Forager's Cottage. Home to retired French homewares dealer Helen May Petschel, the 1930s bungalow comes alive at the turn of the seasons; berries and foliage from the gardens offer a seemingly endless supply of earthy arrangements, the muted tones of which marry well with the rustic interiors of this unassuming, yet curiously charming cottage. 'The foliage outside at this time of year is so beautiful; I can't resist bringing it inside,' notes Helen, setting a kettle on the 20-year-old Falcon range for the first cup of the day.

Nestled among a forest of trees and surrounded by wildlife, the traditional Australian weatherboard cottage with its terracotta roof is steeped in history, with original features fiercely preserved by Helen and her unwavering loyalty to the property's origins. Even the decor has seen little in the way of change over the four decades the 65-year-old has lived here, with Helen preferring the traditions of yesteryear over a more modern way of living. 'I love old things, I love European decor, and the more rural primitive it is, the more it attracts me,' she explains. 'Everything I purchase is from the past. Naturally, I need a fridge, washing machine and oven, but I use old mixing bowls and crockery and eat with old cutlery. My Arabia Ware dinner set was the first modern purchase I made back in 1979 and I still use it today.' Authentic, rustic and useful define Helen's approach to the decoration and styling of her home; pieces with a lifetime of memories fill every nook and cranny. 'Some say I was born in another era; I think they are right,' concedes Helen.

Perhaps the most bewitching space within the cottage is the kitchen, a charm-filled room where vintage cupboards, their age betrayed by weathered patinas, stand like pillars against a backdrop of faded wall paint. Old pots and pans jostle for space alongside a stack of well-worn chopping boards, while jars of bottled fruits add a hint of autumnal colour. Helen chose freestanding antique furniture instead of a commercial fitted kitchen when she bought the property, along with late husband Steve, and has enjoyed moving things around over the years. 'In 42 years, this little room has seen a few furniture changes but with little cost,' she says. 'Selling a piece for another has always been my rule. The kitchen is the heart of my home and the first to greet guests.' An original larder stands as stoically as the day it was built in 1930, with wooden shelving home to Helen's utensils on the left and food on the right. 'It's such a simple design, which I feel hasn't dated in the 94 years since it was built,' observes Helen. 'There's enough room between the shelves to slip a small folding ladder for access to the top shelf. If I had to design the kitchen now, this would be the very larder I'd choose. It's built like a tank and has enough room on top for the creative mind to play.'

Every item of furniture, every pot, pan and utensil, holds memories for Helen, a connection to a person or time that has left an indelible mark. Hers is the epitome of meaningful decor. One such piece is an antique dresser, a Christmas gift from husband Steve, which stands on one side of the kitchen, a reminder of her late partner and home to treasured kitchenware collected over a lifetime. 'The dresser reminds me of Beatrix Potter books,' says Helen. 'It holds my collection of old wares, butter moulds, breadboards, earthenware jugs (pitchers) and bowls, all from Europe, of course. When you collect old things, you can't waste space, so on the

MEANINGFUL DECOR An array of vintage European kitchenalia collected by Helen fills an antique dresser, a gift from her late husband Steve, including bottled fruit preserved from the property's orchard, vintage butter moulds, a ceramic rabbit made by renowned French earthenware producers La Faïencerie de Gien, cutlery and pottery bowls from France, and a Georgian pewter kettle gifted by a friend.

PURE CEYLON
TEA
PACKED
1 kg

top are my butter churn, copper saucepans and a copper pot with a blacksmith handle. Underneath its sliding doors, you'll find all my baking tins and cake racks.'

Only the second generation to occupy the cottage, which is on the edge of a town in Victoria, southeastern Australia, Helen has a deep affinity for her 'humble' dwelling; it is a sanctuary that has remained steadfast through much heartache. In 2001, the couple lost their 19-year-old son Phil to a brain aneurysm and in 2021 Helen's husband of 41 years, Steve, passed away. Born in England, Helen is no stranger to difficult times; the daughter of nomadic parents with little money, she spent an unsettled childhood moving from place to place, often living in caravans and never having a house to call home. A brief, yet happy time spent living with her grandfather in Broad Chalke, Wiltshire, was to have the greatest influence on Helen's passion for vintage European wares and English cottage decor. 'I loved this cottage as it reminded me of my English heritage and my grandfather's Tudor cottage in rural Wiltshire', explains Helen. 'I am strongly connected to my home; it feels untouched by time and reminds me of my English life as a child.'

The cottage's original features lend an otherworldly feel to its rooms; it seems immune to the passage of time, a weathered charm enveloping every corner. Helen still recalls the day she first saw the cottage. 'It was like walking into a time capsule,' she recalls. 'Everything was as it was in 1930; nothing had been modernized in any way. It had an original old wood stove, which is still here today, a claw-foot bathtub, an old wooden draining board with enamel sink and lead splashback, and even one of the light globes had "candle power" printed on it.' The same enamel sink, although now with a pressed tin splashback instead of lead, and brass taps, is still in the scullery, but once avoided a devastating demise. 'When we bought the cottage in 1982, it needed a lot of work before we could move in, so we rented while my husband did up the cottage,' recalls Helen. 'I went into hospital to have our son and when I got home, the little sink that once stood in the kitchen was missing. My husband had replaced it with a stainless-steel sink and brown porcelain taps; I was devastated! But years later, I found it in his sister's shed and was so excited, I picked it up and brought it home.' Knowing how much the sink meant to Helen, Steve agreed to turn the cottage's little washroom into a scullery, and so, 38 years later, the sink was reinstated in its rightful home. A testament to Helen's devotion to preserving the heritage of her cottage, the antique sink and its story of survival continues to bring her great joy. 'The kitchen and adjoining scullery are my favourite rooms; I enjoy doing the washing up in here, at my little lost sink, surrounded by old bits and pieces I've found over the years. I feel the presence of yesteryear in here.'

Pine cones will need collecting to start the evening fire later – one of many simple chores from which Helen derives great joy. 'The smell of pine and the sound of the wind in the trees is what I love about this season,' she says. Contentment is found in the simplicity of her home and the small, yet significant moments that take place there. Helen's interiors exude a raw and rudimentary charm, where sustenance can be found in abundance and a lifetime of collected treasures illustrates a love of authentic vintage design. Though it may not be polished, Helen's little bungalow will forever be a place of unfiltered succour. 'This cottage has hugged us through tragedy and heartache,' she says. 'I look at its cracks and original paint and though it could be easily fixed, I choose not to. I'm only too happy to age inside her walls; we are a comfort to each other.'

ORIGINAL FEATURES An old enamel sink, original to the cottage, with a wooden draining board and green pressed tin splashback, add period charm to the scullery (opposite). The kitchen (overleaf) features a stunning antique cupboard with hand-etched glazed doors. These were originally taken from a captain's quarters on a sailing ship and are estimated to be around 130 years old.

TEA

TEA
RICE
FLOUR
SUGAR
OFFEE
Falcon
110

NOSTALGIC CURIOS A collection of 1930s kitchen canisters creates a focal point above a 20-year-old Falcon range cooker (opposite), complete with copper kettle. Either side of the canisters sit two vintage American oil lamps, also from the 1930s. An 1860s lithograph, depicting three children rescuing a bird, adds a whimsical touch to this characterful space in the kitchen. Preserved apricots and plums from Helen's orchard sit by a window (above).

ANTIQUES & PATINA In the dining room (above), an old seamstress's worktable is repurposed as a dining table and set against Dulux's 'Vintage Green' on the walls. Antiques and heirlooms fill Helen's home (opposite), from earthenware containers and cane furniture on the verandah to a chest of drawers and antique headboards in one of the bedrooms (bottom left and page 206). In the living room (overleaf) Dulux's 'Antique Green' enhances the heritage ambience.

CREATE

CURIOUS CORNERS Antique cutlery from France shares cupboard space with vintage butter moulds and European pottery (above), while an old typewriter, a gift from a friend, sits on a vintage plantation desk in the hallway (opposite top left). Helen enjoys collecting nature finds from her garden and the surrounding wooded area (opposite top right and bottom left). In the bathroom (opposite bottom right), a vintage vanity unit made of sandalwood brings charm to the space.

BYLES
THE

A Miscellany of Colour & Pattern

It is almost inconceivable that Lloyd Hodgkinson's home once contained just a few items of furniture. Now an exuberant cornucopia of original art and striking antiques and a wellspring of pattern and colour, the 1930s home looked very different nine years ago when 39-year-old Lloyd and his husband David first bought the property, in Brisbane, Queensland, Australia.

Yet it is these humble beginnings that have shaped Lloyd's profoundly meaningful approach to the design of his home. 'When we first moved into our home, the only furniture we owned was two really uncomfortable suede sofas, a bed, bookcase and a $30 plastic dining table,' recalls Lloyd. 'We were both in our early thirties and had previously lived in a tiny rented apartment with not much room for furniture. It was a period of growth and learning for us, where every piece of furniture and every corner of our home held a story of resourcefulness and perseverance.'

Fast-forward almost a decade and the couple's home has evolved into a delectable feast for the eyes, with a myriad of curious corners and attention-grabbing objets d'art set against a fearless colour palette of yellow, blue and green. The plastic dining table has been replaced with an arguably superior antique counterpart, while spartan sofas and other makeshift pieces have been switched out for more decorative, characterful items. Quietly amassed over almost two decades, many of Lloyd and David's treasured pieces have waited years for their moment to shine. 'For the past 18 years, my husband and I have been collecting art and objects, much of which were boxed up until we purchased our first home,' says Lloyd. 'One of the most valuable lessons we've learned is patience. Decorating our home didn't happen all at once due to budget constraints, but this approach gave us the opportunity to focus on each item individually. Waiting until we could afford what we truly desired allowed us to curate a space that feels both personal and fulfilling.'

There is a dynamism to the modest two-bedroom period property, proving that size is no barrier to creating individual interiors. Antique pieces are married with more contemporary finds, enveloping its occupants in a blend of old and new. The couple's extensive art collection brings vigour to every room, instinctively drawing the eye in and over an eclectic mix of genres, including old engravings and portraits and more contemporary works. Many of the pieces come from the couple's travels, including a collection of vintage miniature portraits displayed in the primary bedroom, accrued over ten years and found mostly in antiques stores overseas. The key to collecting and curating an art collection, says Lloyd, is to trust your gut. 'When I come across a piece I love, I don't hesitate to acquire it,' explains Lloyd. 'I'm not overly concerned about finding the perfect spot for it immediately; there's always an empty wall or space somewhere. What excites me is the eclectic blend that emerges from collecting diverse pieces of art. Each artwork brings its own character and charm, contributing to a collection that reflects our evolving tastes and interests.'

Lloyd's predilection for colour and pattern is intrinsically linked to his background in interior design. 'I simply could not live without colour and

COLOUR CHARISMA Verdant green cabinets painted in 'Jungle Adventure' by Dulux create colourful impact in the kitchen, where Calacatta Viola Italian marble adds a distinctive aesthetic to countertops. A roman blind (shade) in 'Le Marche Blanc' fabric by Pierre Frey adds a whimsical touch to the space.

HENRI SAMUEL
Billy Baldwin
JANSEN
MARIO BUATTA
INSPIRED DESIGN
INTERIORS
VALENTINO

pattern; for me, their lack of presence would render a space void of any personality,' explains Lloyd. 'I think environments that are vibrant and expressive, filled with a richness of colour, texture and pattern, bring a sense of joy, comfort and perhaps even inspiration.'

Perhaps the most striking of all the rooms is the yellow living and dining area; bold as it is bright, the space, once a 'blank, dull canvas', unapologetically commands attention. Panelled walls painted in Dulux 'Sunbound' are offset with blue and green accents. Lloyd defies the often held notion that yellow is a 'difficult' colour to live with. 'Some say they love the yellow but could never live with it and I think, but why? It is almost like a neutral in the sense that you can add almost any accent colour to it. I think if you are going to commit to a bright colour, it needs to work both during the day and in the evening. "Sunbound" is bright and joyful during the day, but at night, with beautiful soft lighting, the room glows.'

A custom-made green fringed sofa sits below striking artwork by Melbourne-based artist Anna Fitzpatrick, and is paired with a vintage French occasional chair, reupholstered in 'Citron Squiggle' from Colefax and Fowler. Completing the lively scene is a large armchair that Lloyd found on Facebook Marketplace and had recovered in 'Rockbird' fabric by GP & J Baker.

One of the biggest changes when renovating was the transformation of the dated 1960s kitchen into a contemporary space where, again, colour is king. Green cabinets in Dulux's 'Jungle Adventure' contrast strikingly with Calacatta Viola marble countertops, with copper pots adding a warm accent. Blue and white porcelain serveware fills a glazed cabinet, along with a vintage Tiffany & Co. pumpkin soup tureen and a selection of pieces acquired over many years from antiques stores and dealers. The bold colour choice was inspired by a visit to friend and fellow interior designer Anna Spiro's Melbourne home. 'The visit came at a pivotal time as we were on the verge of renovating our kitchen and bathroom, debating between a neutral or colourful palette,' recalls Lloyd. 'Anna's home made a profound impression on us. Seeing her bold use of colour was inspiring, and it solidified our decision to opt for a bright colour scheme. We adore our green kitchen.' The kitchen not only fulfils Lloyd's need for vibrancy in his home but is also key to the couple's love of cooking and entertaining. 'My husband David is a keen cook and known for his culinary prowess among friends and family!' says Lloyd.

It is in the appreciation of even the smallest details that Lloyd gleans the most joy from his home, never more evident than when the couple is planning an evening of entertaining. 'We love to entertain, it's a big part of our lives, and we want our guests to have a memorable experience, so no detail is overlooked,' explains Lloyd. 'Over the years we have collected many beautiful table settings and table linen, and we enjoy mixing and matching these to create an individual look. Linen is pressed, flowers arranged, and the flatware polished. For as long as I can remember, I've enjoyed setting the table, so this process is very much enjoyed.'

There is no single space in the couple's home that Lloyd favours over any other; each space has its own idiosyncratic undertone. 'Our home is a testament to our shared experiences and resilience, so to be honest, every space brings us joy; each room holds a special significance, offering a sense of sanctuary.' And is that not the ultimate goal when designing our home interiors? To create pockets of joy across disparate spaces, each one offering something distinct, is truly the key to an authentic and meaningful home.

VIBRANT DESIGN A bountiful energy fills the living room, with Dulux's 'Yellow Sunbound' on the walls and a custom-made green sofa in 'Sahara Racing Green' fabric by Kirkby Design. Artwork by Melbourne-based artist Anna Fitzpatrick, specially commissioned by Lloyd and his husband, creates a striking focal point above the sofa.

OFFICE AESTHETIC Calming blue walls in Dulux's 'Black Drop' bring serenity to Lloyd's office, which features an original Swedish still-life painting from Vintage Art Room and a French Restoration-style pedestal desk (circa 1900) from Sydney-based The Vault (above). The office is also home to a striking writing bureau (opposite top right). The primary bedroom features a display of miniature portraits, an ornate storage cabinet and a distinctive mirror (all shown opposite).

DAVID HICKS
LIVING WITH DESIGN
HOUSE & GARDEN'S BEST IN DECORATION
Marella Agnelli | The Last Swan
Suzy Menkes THE WINDSOR Style
SISTER PARISH

CHARMED LIFE
IRIS ORIGO
IRIS ORIGO
CHANEL
PRINCE EDDY
GRACE A MEMOIR
VIVIENNE WESTWOOD
SISTER PARISH
FACEHUNTER

INTENTIONAL DECORATION A suzani bedspread sourced from Najaf Rugs adds vibrancy to the guest room, where 'Braidwood' by Porter's Paints adorns the walls and an antique mid-20th-century pendant light from Melbourne-based Miguel Meirelles Antiques brings an element of vintage drama to the space (above and opposite). Fabric in 'Seaweed Lattice – Azure' from London-based Soane Britain features on a roman blind (shade) in this room.

DISTINGUISHED DESIGN Blousy blooms adorn a fabric headboard in the guest room, upholstered in 'Le Grand Corail – Rouge Fond Crème' from French fabric brand Braquenié (above). The primary bedroom (opposite and overleaf) features walls painted in 'Ceylonese' by Dulux, and a collection of antique engravings. The large nude artwork above the bed is by Brisbane-based artist Sheryl Whimp.

HENRY 'CHIPS' CHANNON
HENRY 'CHIPS' CHANNON
THE DIARIES 1938–43
HOLKHAM
REX WHISTLER

THE NAKED SHOT
YOUR SALON BE
FACEHUNTER
VIDAL
COOK EAT REPEAT NIGELLA LAWSON
SISTER PARISH
SISTER PARISH
The Life of the Legendary American Interior Designer

Elle's Address Book

ACCESSORIES
Alice Palmer & Co
alicepalmer.co

Amuse la Bouche
amuselabouche.com

Att Pynta
attpynta.com

Elizabeth Hay
elizabethhaydesign.com

Etsy
etsy.com

The Future Kept
thefuturekept.com

The Hambledon
thehambledon.com

Home Barn
homebarnshop.co.uk

Ian Snow
iansnow.com

Issy Granger
issygranger.com

Liberty
libertylondon.com

Maison Brocante
maisonbrocante.co.uk

Maison Flâneur
maisonflaneur.com

Muddled Vintage
muddledvintage.co.uk

My Little Wish
mylittlewish.com

Rose & Grey
roseandgrey.co.uk

Slowdown Studio
slowdownstudio.com

Sourced By Holly
sourcedbyholly.co.uk

Wicklewood
wicklewood.com

ANTIQUES & VINTAGE
Alto Stile
altostile.com

eBay
ebay.co.uk

The Hoarde
thehoarde.com

IOTA
iotaedit.com

KEPT London
keptlondon.com

Mason & Painter
masonandpainter.com

Pamono
pamono.co.uk

Raffan Kelaher & Thomas
rkta.com.au

Rustique
rustique.uk

Selency
selency.co.uk

Tat London
tat-london.co.uk

Vinterior
vinterior.co

Vintis
vintis.co.uk

ARCHITECTURAL & HARDWARE
Corston Architectural Detail
corston.com

Dowsing & Reynolds
dowsingandreynolds.com

Fired Earth
firedearth.com

Geleta Doors
geleta-doors.co.uk

House of Antique Hardware
houseofantiquehardware.com

House of Brass
houseofbrass.co.uk

Plaster Ceiling Roses
plasterceilingroses.com

Yester Home
yesterhome.com

Your Tiles
yourtiles.com

ART
French Art Shop
frenchartshop.com

Helmsley
helmsleyandco.com

PSTR Studio
pstrstudio.com

Tarn London
tarnlondon.com

Trove Prints
troveprints.co.uk

Vintage Art Room
vintageartroom.com

The Vintage Poster Co
etsy.com/uk/shop/The VintagePosterCo

Wallflower Vintage Art
etsy.com/uk/shop/ wallflowervintageart

BEDDING
Bedfolk
bedfolk.com

Chalk Pink Linen Company
chalkpinklinencompany.co.uk

DUSK
dusk.com

Piglet in Bed
pigletinbed.com

CERAMICS
Cabana
cabanamagazine.com

Leach Pottery
leachpottery.com

Molde
moldeshop.co.uk

Molleni
molleni.com

Villa Bologna Pottery
villabolognapottery.com

FABRICS & WALLPAPER
Charlotte Gaisford
charlottegaisford.com

Forestland Linen
forestlandlinen.com

Ian Mankin
ianmankin.co.uk

Jane Clayton & Co
janeclayton.co.uk

Lucie Annabel
lucieannabel.com

Molly Mahon
mollymahon.com

Morris & Co
wmorrisandco.com

Ottoline
ottoline.co.uk

Sandberg Wallpaper
sandbergwallpaper.com

Sanderson
sanderson. sandersondesigngroup.com

Tess Newall
tessnewall.com

Warner House
warner-house.com

FURNITURE & SOFT FURNISHINGS
Attica Studios
atticastudios.co.uk

Cornish Bed Company
cornishbeds.co.uk

Flora Soames
florasoames.com

Glassette
glassette.com

Graham and Green
grahamandgreen.co.uk

Heal's
heals.com

Neptune
neptune.com

OKA
oka.com

Projekti Tyyny
projektityyny.com

Rebecca Udall
rebeccaudall.com

Rowen & Wren
rowenandwren.co.uk

Ruggable
ruggable.com

Sofas & Stuff
sofasandstuff.com

Water Tiger
watertiger.com.au

HIGH STREET
Anthropologie
anthropologie.com

Habitat
habitat.co.uk

H&M Home
hm.com

John Lewis
johnlewis.com

La Redoute
laredoute.com

Laura Ashley
next.co.uk/laura-ashley

Marks & Spencer
marksandspencer.com

Oliver Bonas
oliverbonas.com

Zara Home
zarahome.com

LIGHTING
David Hunt Lighting
davidhuntlighting.co.uk

Jim Lawrence
jim-lawrence.co.uk

Lights & Lamps
lightsandlamps.com

Light-hearted Lamps
lightheartedlamps.co.uk

Original BTC
originalbtc.com

Pooky Lighting
pooky.com

Rothschild & Bickers
rothschildbickers.com

The Soho Lighting Co
soholighting.com

PAINT
Benjamin Moore
benjaminmoorepaint.co.uk

Craig & Rose
craigandrose.com

Dulux
dulux.co.uk
dulux.com.au

Edward Bulmer
edwardbulmerpaint.co.uk

Farrow & Ball
farrow-ball.com

Lick
lick.com

Little Greene
littlegreene.com

Murobond
murobond.com.au

Paint & Paper Library
paintandpaperlibrary.com

Homeowner Credits

Elle Hervin, @elle_the_home_bird
Pages 1, 2, 3, 5, 6, 8–9, 11, 18, 22, 26, 30, 32, 39, 42, 43, 52, 60–1, 63, 69, 77, 79

Roxanne Fregona, @vincent_the_house
Pages 12, 44, 45, 78

Anita Russell, @by_anitarussell
Pages 13, 48, 75, 83, 139, 140, 143–51

Olive & Hugo Guest, @glebehousedevon
Pages 13, 14, 16–7, 19, 21, 22, 25, 29, 46, 50, 51, 55, 66, 67, 70, 74, 81, 121, 122, 125–37

Helen May Petschel, @the_foragers_cottage
Pages 14, 37, 40–1, 54, 55, 59, 193, 194, 196–207

Fern Avenue Antiques, Newcastle-upon-Tyne
Pages 15, 34

Holly Hardy, @sourced_by_holly
Pages 15, 22, 25, 31, 63, 64, 65, 74, 84–5, 87, 88, 90–103

Charlotte Gaisford, @charlottegaisford
Pages 19, 25, 33, 56, 63, 181, 182, 184–91

Kasturi Wren, @wrenandwhippet
Pages 22, 73, 76, 105, 106, 108–19

Griffin Mill Antiques, Stroud
Page 34

Christen Pear, @christenpears
Pages 47, 63, 82, 153, 154, 155, 156–7, 159–69, 171–4, 176–9

Lloyd Hodgkinson, @olivermarkinteriors
Pages 57, 209, 210, 212, 213–19

Photography Credits

Emma Lewis
1–11, 13, 14 (left), 15–21, 22 (top left, bottom left and right), 25–34, 39, 42, 43, 46–52, 55 (top right and bottom), 56, 60–70, 74, 75, 77, 79–103, 121–91

Hannah Puechmarin
14 (right), 22 (top left), 37, 40-1, 54, 55 (top left), 57, 59, 73, 76, 105–19, 193–207, 209–19

Chris Pugh
12, 44, 45, 78

Index

ACKNOWLEDGEMENTS

When I was eight years old, I filled a school exercise book with my first 'novel', dreams of one day becoming an author already percolating in my mind, then aged 12, I designed a 'magazine' on my dad's PC, and here I am, many decades later at 42, with my first published book. Becoming an author has been a lifelong dream that I steadfastly believed would come to fruition one day, but none of this would have been possible without an incredible team alongside me, or the unwavering support of family and friends.

To my brilliant literary agent Megan Staunton, a thousand thank yous for seeing my 'vision' for this book and helping me shape a myriad of ideas into something feasible. To my wonderful publisher Alison Starling, for taking a chance on me, for believing in this book, and for guiding me every step of the way, you have helped make this dream of mine come true, and for that, I will be forever grateful. Huge thanks to my fabulous art director Juliette Norsworthy, editor Scarlet Furness and the whole team at Octopus Books. Immense gratitude to my talented photographers Emma Lewis, in the UK, with whom I had the most joyful time shooting this book, and Hannah Puechmarin, in Australia, who has brought such beauty and sensitivity to these pages. And thank you, of course, to the wonderful homeowners who opened their doors to me, shared their heartfelt stories, and trusted me to encapsulate their beautiful homes within this book.

Finally, to my boys, thank you for your endless love, cuddles and enthusiasm for 'Mummy's book'. Never stop dreaming. To my husband John, my mum Sarah, my brother Stuart, and my wonderful, beautiful friends who have been on this journey with me the whole way, you are everything.

First published in Great Britain in 2025 by
Mitchell Beazley, an imprint of
Octopus Publishing Group Ltd
Carmelite House
50 Victoria Embankment
London EC4Y 0DZ
www.octopusbooks.co.uk
www.octopusbooksusa.com

An Hachette UK Company
www.hachette.co.uk

The authorized representative in the EEA is
Hachette Ireland, 8 Castlecourt Centre, Dublin 15,
D15 XTP3, Ireland (email: info@hbgi.ie)

Distributed in the US by Hachette Book Group
1290 Avenue of the Americas, 4th and 5th Floors
New York, NY 10104

Distributed in Canada by Canadian Manda Group
664 Annette St., Toronto, Ontario,
Canada M6S 2C8

ISBN 978-1-84091-927-1

A CIP catalogue record for this book is available from the British Library.

Printed and bound in China.

10 9 8 7 6 5 4 3 2

Publishing Director: Alison Starling
Art Director: Juliette Norsworthy
Design Assistant: Ella Mclean
Editor: Scarlet Furness
Copy Editor: Caroline West
Senior Production Manager: Peter Hunt

Elle Hervin is a writer and content creator who has turned her passion for interior design and decorating into a full-time job, following the success of her interiors-based Instagram account **@elle_the_home_bird**, which has attracted more than one million followers. It is here that she showcases her distinctive decorating style, incorporating vintage and modern decor, along with innovative and creative design which has transformed an ordinary house into a beautiful yet practical family home.

Elle has always had a love of interior design, but it became a transformative part of her life after she suffered PTSD following the traumatic birth of her third son, in which she nearly lost her life. A passion for thrifting and sourcing second-hand and vintage homewares became a kind of therapy and helped Elle overcome trauma. She is a huge advocate for creating spaces which are not only reflective of the homeowner as a person, but which also bring about feelings of joy in every single room. *The Home Bird* is her first book.

Endpapers: 'Folk Flower' wallpaper by Tess Newall